The Star Wars Conspiracy:
Hidden Occult and Illuminati Symbolism of Aliens & the New Age

ISAAC WEISHAUPT

For more on Fair Use see:
http://www.copyright.gov/fls/fl102.html

Notwithstanding the provisions of sections 106 and 106A, the fair use of a copyrighted work, including such use by reproduction in copies or phonorecords or by any other means specified by that section, for purposes such as criticism, comment, news reporting, teaching (including multiple copies for classroom use), scholarship, or research, is not an infringement of copyright. In determining whether the use made of a work in any particular case is a fair use the factors to be considered shall include - (1) the purpose and character of the use, including whether such use is of a commercial nature or is for nonprofit educational purposes; (2) the nature of the copyrighted work; (3) the amount and substantiality of the portion used in relation to the copyrighted work as a whole; and (4) the effect of the use upon the potential market for or value of the copyrighted work. The fact that a work is unpublished shall not itself bar a finding of fair use if such finding is made upon consideration of all the above factors. - See more at:
http://codes.lp.findlaw.com/uscode/17/1/107#sthash.2LC o5Fg5.dpuf

Table of Contents

Foreword

I realize that many of you are reading this in the hopes that I won't show the beloved saga of *Star Wars* in a negative light, and I can assure you that is not my intent. Instead, I hope to continue my life's work of understanding the ways of the "Illuminati" and the occult beliefs hidden in our entertainment. The *Star Wars* tale is one in which we'll see many of the same themes I've covered elsewhere in my other books or on IlluminatiWatcher.com.

When I mention the "Illuminati" I'm not specifically talking about the 1776 Bavarian Illuminati started by Adam Weishaupt (of no relation to the author- my pen name is a pseudonym echoing the website: Illuminati Watcher = Isaac Weishaupt). Instead, I'm discussing an umbrella group of people who all seem to be on the same team. This team seeks to evolve humanity into a new world through an occult belief system. Whether or not the reader wants to believe that this group is "evil" or not is to be decided. I can say that it's not always crystal clear, but for the most part it seems that many have fallen under the hypnotic trance of Luciferianism which is in opposition to my personal beliefs. Many theorists subscribe to this idea, but the purpose for it all is where we start to divert.

For example, I feel that the driving purpose behind all of this is to expose us to the occult belief in worshipping the fallen angel of Lucifer. The belief in aliens will be one in which they'll expect everyone to subscribe to, such that they can invite other fallen angels and demons who disguise themselves as aliens into our world.

In this research project I'll provide minimal background on some of the characters and groups that are part of this "Illuminati" umbrella in order for the reader to be able to get the basic premise of the theory. I don't intend to bog the reader down with some of the fine details unless it is necessary to understand the ideas being presented.

The progression of the *Star Wars*-Illuminati theory takes the reader through explorations of occult doctrine, including the concepts of duality (light vs. dark), Joseph Campbell's "Hero's Journey," Aleister Crowley's Thelema beliefs in magick and the New Age powers of the mind with Blavatsky's super-man with hidden powers. The global consciousness is demonstrated with the science fiction agenda to destroy Christianity while programming the concept of an impersonal God that exists in a future without organized religion. Transhumanism takes the center stage as we see the possibilities to keep the body alive through augmentation of technology. This technology is demonstrated as once existing "long ago and far away;" akin to the mysteries of Atlantis and Lemuria that many New Age occultists have desired to pursue.

Like other works of science fiction, *Star Wars* shows us a world of fantasy, but the truth behind it is that the "Illuminati" want us to pursue this fantasy to the point of fanatic belief. The genre of science fiction typically shows us an alternate version of reality devoid of religion, and this is echoed as the global consciousness' version of creation with the Force. Sci-fi is also instrumental in supporting theories of occultists who suggest that there are hidden, latent powers within all of mankind that will someday be unlocked, and that is the journey we take with young Anakin and Luke Skywalker.

The concept of bringing "balance to the Force" is a veiled mission statement of occult beliefs. We'll find out why this is the case because destroying the dark side would indeed *not* bring balance since the dark and light would need to be in a state of equilibrium in order for there to be true balance.

Follow along as we enter into the dark Abyss of the Kabbalah Tree of Life where the hidden sephirot of Da'ath resides. This realm is one in which the initiate must be prepared to enter before losing one's self entirely; just like we witness with Anakin's transition into Darth Vader...

Let me conclude the foreword by stating that I'm also a *Star Wars* fan (I'm not sure who *isn't* at this point), but I'm not so entrenched with it that I understand some of the nuances and extra books, characters, etc. from the extended *Star Wars* Universe and whatnot. I've simply been a fan of the film series since the beginning and enjoy the same symbolism, archetypes, action figures, and imagery that has been given to us since the release of *A New Hope* in 1977.

When you begin to research the universe of *Star Wars* you'll quickly learn that there is an overwhelming breadth (and depth) of resources available and although I haven't delved as far as the options allowed, the thread of theory is intertwined all the way to the deepest recesses of *Star Wars* fantasy one can entertain. This project is not going to analyze the *Star Wars* films in a chronological or sequential fashion, but instead it will take the reader on a journey of occult history while injecting different messages and symbols from the *Star Wars* tales.

Spoilers lay ahead…

Chapter 1
George Lucas: On the Path

Before we start decoding *Star Wars,* I'd like to pull out a few considerations surrounding the creation of the films. This is part of the argument that there is a certain spirit of influence that has connections to Luciferianism and the beliefs of the Illuminati.

The creative force behind the *Star Wars* phenomenon can generally be attributed to the award winning filmmaker George Lucas. Not only did he succeed in making some of the most popular films of all time; but he also proved to be a successful entrepreneur by founding Lucasfilm and Industrial Light & Magic (ILM).

In 2012 he sold Lucasfilm to Disney for 4 *billion* dollars. [1]

When we look deeper into the hidden meanings and symbolism behind George Lucas and his ventures, it seems there *may* be an occult influence. For instance, (even though this is a very shallow example), George Lucas' name suggests Luciferian attitudes if we consider that the name "Lucas" is closely related to the name of Lucifer: the light bearer and fallen angel.

Obviously the man did not choose this name, nor does it imply that he is inherently "evil", but it does beg the question if something is lurking beneath the surface as the inspiration for these infamous tales he managed to piece together once you look at all of the evidence.

Another idea to consider is that the Lucasfilm production company is based out of the Letterman Digital Arts Center in San Francisco, CA. This division of the Walt Disney Empire is actually located inside of the Presidio- a former military complex that *also* houses the Industrial Light & Magic (ILM) visual effects company.

Why does that raise any kind of concern? Well, if you consider the connections of the entertainment industry (particularly Disney) with the military industrial complex, it seems something could very well be awry...

The Presidio was alleged to be a location in which certain mind control operations were conducted- and worse yet sexual abuse of children at a daycare center. In 1987, the US Army decided to demolish a day care center after an investigation into the claims that as many as 60 children were sexually abused while they were in the care of the Presidio Child Development Center. [2] The investigation charged minister and CDC worker Gary Hambright with multiple sexual related crimes, although he made some very strange responses that suggested others may have been involved:

"I cannot understand why these allegations and falsehoods have been, directed solely at me."- Gary Hambright [3]

The reason I bring this up is because there is an article allegedly written by San Jose Mercury News' Linda Goldston called *Army of the Night* that reveals potential connections with Michael Aquino on this Presidio case. I include the term "allegedly" because I wasn't able to confirm the validity of this article as of this writing. I was indeed able to confirm that Linda

Goldston was a journalist at San Jose Mercury News who specialized in the fate of children; although this exact article was only retrievable at a website that wasn't San Jose Mercury News. [3]

If we consider the article to be true, then I'd like to point out some ideas that we can apply here (without going *too* deep into things). Goldston mentions that a Lt. Col. Michael Aquino was being investigated in connections with the child abuse, and this is interesting because he was a prominent Satanist and started the Temple of Set. This group of practicing Satanists seek to utilize black magic in the purpose of self-deification, all the while worshipping Lucifer as a true hero of mankind.

Now, that doesn't mean that Satanists are molesting children, but it does draw some interesting parallels, as Linda Goldston points out in her article:

The Army did not suspend his clearance when he joined the Church of Satan, founded by Anton LaVey, in 1969. Nor when Aquino founded his own satanic church in 1975. Nor when Aquino while on a NATO tour of Europe in 1982 performed a satanic ritual in the Westphalian castle that had been used as an occult sanctuary by Heinrich Himmler's SS elite in Nazi Germany. Nor did the Army move to suspend Aquino's top security clearance during the sex abuse investigation. "The nature of the investigation that prompted the search of his house, and I understand some of his belongings were taken by police, really is a question for the San Francisco Police Department," Maj. Greg Rixon, spokesman at the Pentagon said Aquino, who now works as a program analyst at the Army Reserve Personnel Center in St Louis, has vehemently denied ever meeting or having in his house the young girl who has alleged he abused her. He unsuccessfully tried to have court martial proceedings initiated against Adams-Thompson.

In a Temple of Set newsletter sent out two months after the search of his home, Aquino accused Adams-Thompson, who is an assistant chaplain for the Army, of trumping up the allegations as some sort of Christian vendetta "Also relevant is his profession as a Christian clergyman; I certainly doubt that he would have made such an outrageous accusation against any Lieutenant Colonel who was not known to be a prominent Satanist"

In April, Aquino wrote a four-page letter to the head of a children's advocates group in Southern California warning that "we do not intend to see a replay of what happened in Nazi Germany, when the reluctance of the Jews to challenge those who systematically and falsely accused Judaism of heinous crimes-including the sexual abuse and ritual murder of Christian children- led to violence against them."

Aquino said that the Temple of Set neither prescribes nor tolerates any form of harm, sexual or otherwise, to children or animals. "It is made clear in our membership publications that, should we have any reason to think that a member is engaged in any such activity, he or she will be immediately expelled and reported to the appropriate law enforcement or animal-protection authorities." [3]

How interesting is it that we see Lucas' Industrial Light & Magic company (which was created for the production of *Star Wars*) being housed at the Presidio, which *also* shows us the symbolism of the light bearer of Luciferianism with the lightbulb on their promotional logos?...

Is the Luciferianism of Michael Aqunio's Temple of Set being evoked in the mental abuse of children through mind altering works of entertainment?...

We'll explore more ideas of coordinated mind control and traumatization a bit later as well.

Aquino did in fact believe he was in secession to Aleister Crowley who once stated:

Moreover, the Beast 666 adviseth that all children shall be accustomed from infancy to witness every type of sexual act, as also the process of birth, lest falsehood fog, and mystery stupefy their minds, whose error else might thwart and misdirect the growth of their subconscious system of soul-symbolism. [4]

Another interesting consideration of Lucas is that many of the successful ventures he created would later be absorbed by The Walt Disney Company. Pixar had its roots inside of Lucas' Lucasfilm which would later be acquired by Disney in 2006, which made then-CEO Steve Jobs a very wealthy man since Pixar was bought for $7.4 billion. [5]

As was previously mentioned, Lucasfilm was also picked up by Disney in 2012 for over $4 billion. [6] What's interesting about this power acquisition by Disney is that Lucas found himself in a bit of trouble for telling journalist Charlie Rose that he had sold his:

"...kids... to the white slavers that take these things." [7]

Of course, Lucas would later retract the veracity of these statements and claim that he misspoke, but perhaps he was trying to expose the truth behind one of the largest corporations that is behind a vast majority of our entertainment today...

I believe that Disney is trying to procure tales such as *Star Wars* for its influence on the masses. Lucas once said that he wanted to give the youth a sort of "template" to follow with *Star Wars*, meanwhile Disney is also well known for its ability to influence children. One should also consider that Lucas was partially motivated to write *Star Wars* based on Joseph Campbell's monomyth "Hero's Journey" which brilliantly explained how our modern society is subtlety brainwashed by tales such as this.

We are programmed to pursue our childhood interests and these attitudes are kept intact the rest of our lives. There are entire industries dedicated to keeping this spirit alive. For instance, men continue to be obsessed with sports and athletes well past the appropriate time they should (not to single out or pick on sports fans...).

A good example of this is the fantasy football game many play. If you research Campbell's theories, you'll find more support for this theory (later on in the book he refers to it as *"life potentialities that we never managed to bring to adult realization"*):

> *And so, while husbands are worshiping at their*
> *boyhood shrines, being the lawyers, merchants, or*
> *masterminds*
> *their parents wanted them to be, their wives, even after*
> *fourteen*
> *years of marriage and two fine children produced and*
> *raised, are*
> *still on the search for love—which can come to them*
> *only from*
> *the centaurs, sileni, satyrs, and other concupiscent*
> *incubi of the*
> *rout of Pan, either as in the second of the above-recited*
> *dreams,*
> *or as in our popular, vanilla-frosted temples of the*
> *venereal goddess,*
> *under the make-up of the latest heroes of the screen.* [8]

Before George Lucas starting shooting his first film, he wanted to experiment with a new lens at the 1969 Altamont rock concert. This would prove to be a pivotal moment in the American pop culture legacy of the 1960s when the hippies would come face to face with real horror. Similar to other theories of blood sacrifices being conducted in an occult manner, Altamont may very well have instilled the spirit of occultism into Lucas without his knowing. Demonic forces were definitely present that day so I find it important to understand how Lucas was connected to the event.

16

The lens he wanted to use could capture the stage from over a mile away, and one of his shots would indeed make it onto the Rolling Stones documentary *Gimme Shelter* (it happens when they pan across an exodus of people leaving Altamont with the moon in the background). [9]

Most people are familiar with Altamont as the final death nail in the 1960s hippie movement with the Manson Family murders being the first one. The reason for this is due to an 18-year-old African-American man named Meredith Hunter who was stabbed and beaten to death by the Altamont security guards comprised of Hells Angels bikers. Hunter drew a gun and attempted to get on stage after the Rolling Stones performance of *Sympathy for the Devil*. Interestingly enough, Stones' lead singer Mick Jagger was previously dabbling in occult practices like starring in Satanist Kenneth Anger's *Invocation of My Demon Brother* along with Manson Family murderer Bobby Beausoleil.

During the Altamont concert, Mick Jagger was attempting to calm the crowd down because they felt something dark and heavy taking over. Before the fatal stabbing, Jagger was referring to their performance of *Sympathy for the Devil* when he told the crowd:

"We always have something very funny that happens when we start that number." [9]

After the Altamont concert, Jagger turned down Kenneth Anger's offer as leading role in *Lucifer Rising*. Jagger apparently felt too close to evil to take on the persona of Lucifer after the Altamont stabbing. Author Joel Selvin confirmed this in *Altamont: The Rolling Stones, the Hells Angels, and the Inside Story of Rock's Darkest Day* when he pointed out the vast difference in their music after the life changing 1969 event:

"Coming face-to-face with its real-life power for destruction was another, and it shook the band to their souls. They would never again risk such fearlessness. Yet it was that exact fearlessness that had given their music such vivid, explosive power. [9]

In *Gimme Shelter* we hear a person in the crowd claim that Jagger's then-girlfriend Marianne Faithfull, was in attendance. The late 60s was a time period when Jagger was influenced by Faithfull; even to the point that she introduced him to the book that inspired Jagger to write *Sympathy for the Devil* (Mikhail Bulgakov's *The Master and Margarita*). [10]

I wrote about their occult obsession in my analysis of *The Rocky Horror Picture Show* in the project entitled: *It's Just a Jump to the Left… The Unauthorized Guide to Occult Symbolism in The Rocky Horror Picture Show*:

The character(s) of Magenta and Columbia were originally slated to be *one* woman. This character was to be played by a woman named Marianne Faithfull who was a major player in the 70s occult works of art. Aleister Crowley devotee Kenneth Anger tapped Marianne Faithfull to play the role of Lilith in his film *Lucifer Rising*. If you read an article from NewDawnMagazine.com, you'll find just how deep into the occult she really was; including her connections with Rolling Stones' Mick Jagger:

Mick Jagger's one time girlfriend Marianne Faithfull described how she and Pallenberg used to sit for hours reading aloud passages from Robert Graves' book The White Goddess and studying the ancient Celtic tree alphabet. In her autobiography Marianne Faithfull claims the gay Anger had a crush on the bisexual Stones' singer which was not reciprocated.

18

When the filmmaker's sexual overtures were rejected he became a bit of a nuisance. One day he turned up at the couple's house in Cheyne Walk, Chelsea and bizarrely threw several books by the 18th century poet and mystic William Blake through the window. Jagger responded in disgust at this stunt by burning all the copies of the occult works that Anger had given him by Crowley and the French occultist Eliphas Levi.

Despite this, Marianne Faithfull got involved in Anger's experimental movie Lucifer Rising, allegedly financially sponsored by Anita Pallenberg, and with a score originally to be composed by Mick Jagger. Initially the Stones' singer was to play the leading role in the film, but he got cold feet and backed out of the project altogether. In the first version, made in 1967, the lead was taken by his brother Chris Jagger. Marianne Faithfull became involved in the second version filmed in 1972 and she agreed to take the part of the demon-goddess Lilith. Faithfull described the baby-slaying Lilith as one of the classic female archetypes and compared her with pagan goddesses such as Diana, Astarte, Ishtar, Aphrodite and Demeter. However, she added:

'From the view of patriarchy, of course, she was the pure incarnation of evil" *(Faithfull by Marianne Faithfull with David Datton, 224).*

Interestingly, the part of the ancient Egyptian god Osiris in the film was played by Donald Cammell, son of Charles Cammell, a friend and biographer of Crowley. The younger Cammell made his own films including the controversial Performance in co-operation with Nic Roeg. It starred Mick Jagger, Anita Pallenberg and the archetypal English actor Edward Fox. Donald Cammell committed suicide in the 1990s.

The shooting of Lucifer Rising took place in Egypt and Faithfull claims that as soon as the crew and cast arrived in the country it was obvious Anger did not know what he was doing as either a film director or a magician. At that stage in her life Faithfull was seriously addicted to heroin and admits she did not know what she was doing on the set either. The whole thing was a recipe for disaster. The last sequence of the film was a winter solstice rite shot at a Neolithic site in Germany. During it, Faithfull managed to fall off a mountain. She somersaulted and landed on her feet without sustaining any injury. This convinced her that her magic was stronger than Anger's. In her autobiography she dismissed him as a "kitsch occultist" and "a witch out of a Hollywood tabloid."

Marianne Faithfull claims that both Mick Jagger and the Stones' lead guitarist Keith Richards were also sceptical about Anger's "satanic hocus-pocus" and did not take any of it seriously. However, after an incident involving the magician at the house in London now shared by Richards and Anita Pallenberg, Faithfull became seriously spooked out. As a result, she believed she was under psychic attack. Allegedly, she wore a clove of garlic around her neck and slept in a circle of lit candles for protection. Whether this paranoid behaviour was connected to her heroin addiction is not known.

One of Marianne Faithfull's tracks on her comeback album Broken English is called 'Witches Song'. She dedicates it as "my ode to the wild pagan woman I know and have always around me." Faithfull says she got the idea for the song after she and Mick Jagger visited an exhibition in Madrid of paintings on the theme of the Witches Sabbath by the Spanish artist Goya. Her autobiography also describes an incident when she and Jagger took LSD before visiting Primrose Hill in North London "where the ancient ley lines are supposed to run" and where modern neo-druids hold their seasonal ceremonies. Under the influence of the acid the couple saw "a great face in the sky" they were convinced was the head of the Celtic giant god Bran. This seems to fit with Faithfull's professed pagan *beliefs. In her autobiography she says she believes not in God the Father, but in the Great Goddess and her consort Pan.*

So it seems that Mick Jagger was tied into some serious "witchery" with his girlfriend who set to play the Magenta/Columbia role. It should also interest the reader to find out that Mick Jagger also wanted to play the role of Dr. Frank N Furter...

To find out that Jagger's "witchy" girlfriend was in attendance only adds to the mystery of what exactly possessed the crowd at Altamont as the concert turned into a scene of murderous rage and LSD-fueled hysteria. Charles Manson claimed that his Family was taken over by a spirit of evil when they exposed themselves to it at the infamous 'Spiral Staircase' in Los Angeles, so it's not so far-fetched to think that Lucas may *also* have been greeted by a spirit of evil at Altamont before he created *Star Wars*.

George Lucas' first full length film was *THX 1138* which shows us a dystopian future with a police state and forced mind altering drugs. The film shows us the Illuminati agenda in that the concept of a cohesive family is suppressed. It also shows us a world in which safety and increased production throughput are the focused efforts of an all too oppressive government.

Some claim that Lucas chose the title of *THX 1138* because of the symmetry on the letters, but one thing that runs common through all occult symbolism is that of numerology. In this practice, mystical meanings are established between numbers and letters. Analyzing *THX 1138* gives us the numerological equivalent to:

$$(T=2) + (H=9) + (X=6) + 1+1+3+8 = 2+9+6+1+1+3+8$$
$$= 30 = 3+0 = 3$$

The number three is important in terms of occult symbolism due to its equivalency to the creative force. I've laid this concept out in *Decoding Illuminati Symbolism: Triangles, Pyramids and the Sun* where we saw the trinities of ancient Egypt as well as Christianity which demonstrate the creative force behind the mother, father, and child. The number three embodies the mystical powers of the heavens and the creative force of manifestation. This is why ceremonial magicians utilize a triangle on the floor in order to conjure a demon into our world. They are manifesting the spirit before they commence with their negotiation of strengths from the entity.

Lucas continued to reference *THX 1138* in many of his most popular films. For example, the "deity" from *THX 1138* known as OMM 0910 appears as the name of the computer operating system in *Star Wars Episode I* known as the "Operational Multisystem Management."

How curious is the fact that OMM 0910 has a numerological equivalence we should consider?

$$6+4+4+9+1=24=6$$

The number six represents the embodiment of evil on multiple levels. Even those that don't believe in a good vs. evil concept can agree that the number six symbolizes the outside forces, or the "other." We see it appear in the Bible as a reference to the Beast in the Book of Revelation with the Antichrist's number of 666. We also see it utilized by the ceremonial magick groups such as the Hermetic Order of the Golden Dawn and Aleister Crowley's Thelemic magick in the *Rituals of the Pentagram and Hexagram* that the practitioner uses to protect their aura. The numbers 5 and 6 are unionized to demonstrate 11 paths on the Kabbalah Tree of Life.

Freeman Fly asserts this number's sinister value in *Weird Stuff: Operation Culture Creation* when he details the symbolism behind 9/11:

Therefore, 9/11 is a compounded number of Satanic value. Going from 9 to 11 on the Tree of Life without the balance of the unity of 10 (Heaven), symbolizes selfish agendas to destroy the lives of many along with the world's sense of security. 9/11 is a Luciferian Symbol of man becoming God. [11]

The number 11 is also associated with the hidden Sephirot on the Tree of Life known as Da'ath (aka Da'at), which the astute reader should already see as another association in the *Star Wars* Universe with Darth Vader. He perfectly demonstrates the "outer" hidden realm of Da'at as well as the symbolism behind the number six. His all-black outfit suggests he is indeed the force behind the planet Saturn which is symbolized as a black cube (which we also see from the outfits of Darth Maul, Count Dooku, Kylo Ren, and Darth Sidius- who looks just like Aleister Crowley at one point). Ancient occultists believed that Saturn was the outer most planet we could see and they labeled it as the force of the "other" which should be embraced as the shadow side.

In *Star Wars Episode II* we see a location called Geonosis (which is a play on the word Gnosis from the Gnostic group of early esoteric Christians). Later in the film we confirm that it resembles the planet of Saturn. Even later on we find out that Count Dooku is here and it is the location of the ritualistic killing games.

Ironically, Count Dooku was played by Sir Christopher Lee, who is known for playing occult type villains such as the corrupted wizard Saruman from *The Lord of the Rings*. He was asked about his occult connections at the University College of Dublin and he admitted to owning *The Devil Rides Out* (a film he starred in) while he also said to have met people that were claiming to be involved with Satanism and black magick. He warned the audience that they shouldn't get involved with occult teachings because they would:

"...not only lose your mind but you'll lose your soul."

How interesting is it that Lee warned of the occult teachings yet played so many roles that employed the usage of such practices?...

Over time, civilizations labeled the number six and the planet Saturn as the opposing, antinomian forces. So it seems entertainment's portrayal of bad guys wearing black is simply another symbolic programming of the "dark side" which embodies "evil." We also see the portrayal of the number six in *Episode IV* with the halls of the Death Star shaped as the black hexagon of Saturn with six sides.

Getting back to Lucas' *THX 1138*, we can see its resemblances to similar tales like *1984* and *Brave New World*. These stories were written by George Orwell and Aldous Huxley (respectively). The purpose of these novels was to show us a world with total government control. In fact, the US government had a project called the Mockingbird Operation which funded the Orwell film of *Animal Farm* which warned of the dangers of communism. Huxley and Orwell were also allegedly close with the Fabian Society and Huxley also spent time with Aleister Crowley in 1930 [12].

Whether it be "thoughtcrimes", psychological operation conditioning, or over-surveillance, these tales show us a dystopian future that we should be cautious of. Lucas' *THX 1138* is similar in its warnings and predictive programming of a future world that we may have caught glimpses of from the science fiction genre in the years since its release.

****

As we progress through the symbolism and hidden messages of *Star Wars*, I ask the reader to keep in mind the influence of arts and entertainment and the true power it wields. No matter what you think of George Lucas and the *Star Wars* tales; it's undeniable that their presence, or *Force*, is felt by everyone. How likely might it be that Lucas was inspired by a Luciferian source without his knowledge?

Could it be that the *Star Wars* tales are merely a retelling of an ancient occult belief; designed to lead the masses astray in the pursuit of a future world in which a global consciousness is steered down a path of self-deification and pursuit of a false teaching from the fallen angel?

Perhaps he tapped into something much more powerful than even he realized...

Chapter 2
Old Religion is the New Religion

The origin of the *Star Wars* tale goes back to George Lucas alongside producer Gary Kurtz as they brainstormed a *Flash Gordon*-esque science fiction film. Lucas would write the screenplay and hand it off to ghostwriter Alan Dean Foster to write the novel. Ultimately, Lucas came up with the *Star Wars* story we are all familiar with, along with Gary Kurtz's feedback, which contains belief in a one world consciousness and hidden energy fields known as the Force.

We already explored a bit of George Lucas, but Gary Kurtz also needs examined to see what inspirations may have led him to contribute to the esoteric aspects of the Force.

Gary Kurtz was a friend of Lucas and worked with him on the 1973 film *American Graffiti*. Remarkably enough, this film starred Mackenzie Phillips- daughter of seminal 60s folk band The Mamas & the Papas' John Phillips. I state this as odd because not only did Gary Kurtz legally have to make Mackenzie under his legal guardianship to be in the film (due to California law at the time); but there are considerable occult connections with John Phillips to recognize.

First, the most disturbing consideration is that John Phillips was alleged by Mackenzie to have sexually abused her. In 2009 she told Oprah Winfrey that her father injected her with heroin and cocaine when she was 11 years old, and in her memoir *High On Arrival*, she would relay her forgiveness of her father's misdoings. [13]

To get deeper into the occult links- we have to examine Adam Gorightly's *The Shadow Over Santa Susana* to find out that John Phillips was involved with alleged sex parties at 10050 Cielo Drive (the location of the infamous Sharon Tate murders at the hands of the Manson Family).

In *Doris Day: Her Own Story*, Terry Melcher was quoted saying:

"...(*The Manson Family) murders had something to do with the weird film Polanski had made, and the equally weird people who were hanging around the house. I knew they had been making a lot of homemade sadomasochistic-porn movies there with quite a few recognizable Hollywood faces in them. The reason I knew was that I had gone out with a girl named Michelle Phillips, one of the Mamas and Papas, whose ex-husband, John Phillips, was the leader of the group. Michelle told me she and John had had dinner one night, to discuss maybe getting back together, and afterward he had taken her up to visit the Polanski's in my old house. Michelle said that when they arrived there, everyone in the house was busy filming an orgy and that Sharon Tate was part of it. That was just one of the stories I had heard about what went on in my former house.*" [14]

One of Charles Manson's ambitions were to take his "Family" out to the desert of Death Valley. He infamously holed up there at Barker Ranch while he taught his members more of his philosophy. Part of this was that the desert is one of the greatest teachers there is. This same principle is echoed in Paulo Coelho's *The Alchemist*, which supports many of the occult and New Age theories with Crowley principles hidden within. We

28

see the desert's ability to teach characters of *Star Wars* like Luke Skywalker when we are first shown his house on the deserts of Tatooine.

This desert planet is also the home of his father-Anakin Skywalker. In *Episode IV* we hear Luke telling C3PO:

> *"If there's a bright center to the universe, you are on the planet the furthest from."*

The purpose of this statement could very well imply that the desert planet of Tatooine is analogous to the planet of Saturn which was at one time believed to be the planet furthest from the sun, and thus the inspiration and source of wisdom for many occultists who seek to learn from the planet that represented Set and referred to as the "Other."

Granted we are looking at six degrees of separation between George Lucas and Charles Manson (Manson-John Philips-Mackenzie Philips-Gary Kurtz-George Lucas); but it's another interesting connection between Hollywood and Charles Manson, who was quite possibly connected to the darkest underbelly of satanic cults in the Illuminati.

Another idea to consider is that we have heard theories of Disney's attempts at grooming child stars into mind controlled tools of the Illuminati who would later seem to have mental breakdowns to support the theory (e.g. Britney Spears, Lindsay Lohan, etc.).

For example, Cathy O'Brien asserts that she was a victim of the Project MONARCH mind control programming in her tragically horrifying book *Trance: Formation of America*. She details the importance of utilizing Disney in the big agenda through blurring the lines of reality and fantasy in tales such as *Cinderella* and *Fantasia*. She says that many are programmed with Disney's traumatic story lines such as murdering the parent figures- a concept we'll discuss later that occurs in

Star Wars. We can also see the fact that many people become *obsessed* with Disney, even through adulthood, almost as if it is a form of brainwashing.

Cathy O'Brien asserts that there is indeed a connection between the CIA's mind control MKULTRA program along with Disney:

"During Christmas vacation of 1974, my father flew us all to Disney World by route of Tampa, Florida. Ignorant of geography, it did not occur to me that Tampa was out of the way to Disney World until my father drove the rented van to the gates of MacDill Air Force Base. Military personnel met me there and escorted me into the base TOP SECRET high tech mind-control conditioning facility for "behavioral modification" programming. [15]

When considering George Lucas' religious beliefs, he once stated that he is "Buddhist Methodist." However, when looking further into Gary Kurtz, we find out that he is a Latter Day Saint Mormon. [16] This faith claims to be Christian in nature, but many are quick to point out the occult connections at the inceptions of this religion- from Freemasonry, to ancient Egyptian paganism, and possibly witchcraft and magick. The faith was founded on Joseph Smith's alleged experiences as a black magician and sorcerer who evoked spirits that relayed the principles of the LDS religion through the Book of Mormon. If this sounds familiar; it could be because famed occultist Aleister Crowley started his Thelema religion based on the spiritual evocation of Aiwass- another disembodied spirit similar to Smith's Moroni angel.

As we'll discuss later- the concept of transhumanism is evident in *Star Wars*, which is an idea that is also supported by the Mormon Transhumanist Association- a group of LDS members that believe their faith shares the same ideals as transhumanism and the advent of a new technologically supplanted revolution of humanity (*the LDS church does not officially affiliate itself with this group).

There is another interstellar sci-fi fantasy tale written by an LDS Mormon called *Battlestar Galactica*. This tale is full of LDS references, including the idea of a distant world from "a long time ago on a planet far away" known as Kobol (Joseph Smith refers to it as "Kolob"- the galactic center of God's creation). The writer of this story, Glen Larson, allegedly wanted to title the show *Galactica*, but was convinced to add the word "Battlestar" to the title in order to capitalize on *Star Wars*' success- further emphasizing the connections between the occult and pursuing contact with our distant birthing from the stars.

Coincidentally, *Star Wars Episode I: The Phantom Menace* takes place on the planet of Naboo, while there is also a town called Nauvoo in Indiana that is revered by LDS Mormons since Joseph Smith was the mayor (and gave it the name of Nauvoo), until his imprisonment and murder in 1844.

Another interesting connection to consider is that Kurtz lost most of his *Star Wars* earnings in his financial backing of *Return to Oz*- a film disaster coopted by Disney (*recall earlier that we talked about the connections of Disney and the blurring of reality-fantasy through the tales Cathy O'Brien asserts in her experiences, which includes *The Wizard of Oz*). [17]

Getting back on the track of Kurtz and his LDS contributions to *Star Wars*, we can see that the Force is utilized by Jedi Knights, which is analogous to the LDS priesthood. LDS President Gordon B. Hinckley once spoke of the LDS priesthood as follows:

"*There is no power on the earth like it. Its authority extends beyond life, through the veil of death, to the eternities ahead. It is everlasting in its consequences.*" –Gordon B. Hinckley, 1984 [16]

The LDS believe the priesthood is an energy from which all of the earth and heavens was created-similar to the Force.

We see the quest for immortality from the LDS that believe we are all truly eternal beings; which we witness in the *Star Wars* films when the Jedi Knights continue to appear from beyond the grave, such as Obi-Wan Kanobi as he guides Luke Skywalker into the world of the Jedi. LDS prophet Lorenzo Snow once said:

"As man now is, God once was. As God now is, man may be."
[16]

The concept of immortality is one shared by many occultists; including the aforementioned transhumanists. The transhumanism movement seeks to extend life much further than we can comprehend. The occultists seem to think of transhumanism as an elixir of life for immortality which fits in nicely with the Mormon Transhumanist Association and the immortality of the Jedi Knights.

The premise behind *Star Wars* revolves around a mysteriously hidden energy referred to as "The Force." This metaphysical energy is tapped into by those trained in the arts of white or black magick since one could harness the "good" energy of the light side, or the "evil" energy of the dark side. In *Episode IV: A New Hope* we hear Obi-Wan Kenobi describe it as:

"…an energy field created by all living things."

If you want to know *who* can tap into this energy; there are two considerations to be made. Initially, it was intended for *everyone* to be able to utilize the Force. However, when *The Phantom Menace* was released, it was revealed that microorganisms referred to as midi-chlorians were the key to connection to the Force. The

32

more midi-chlorians one possesses; the more sensitive they are to the Force.

What is interesting about the Force is that it wasn't in the original scripts, which begs the question of how Lucas got motivated to incorporate this idea (I believe that it was due to Kurtz's spirituality):

The Force wasn't mentioned in the script's first drafts. It first appeared in the Second Draft of January 1975, a year after Lucas started writing. People in early scripts occasionally say 'May the force of others be with you' instead of 'Good luck,' but what force is never mentioned. Lucas himself didn't begin expounding the Force until well after the film's release. In 1977, he was still saying vaguely, 'The Force is really a way of seeing, it's a way of being with life.' All evidence suggests that the secret of Star Wars' extraordinary longevity and the fidelity of its following, indeed the basis of George Lucas's later near-guru status, was an afterthought. [17]

Lucas also described it similarly as:

The act of living generates a force field, an energy. That energy surrounds us.... There is a giant mass of energy in the universe that has a good side and a bad side. We are part of the Force because we generate the power that makes the Force live. When we die, we become part of that Force, so we never really die. [18]

As you'll see in this section, the Force is merely a rehashing of the pagan belief in an impersonal, universal version of God as a cosmic consciousness.

The inspiration for the tag line of "*May the Force be with you*" also has interesting origins. Some claim it is a play on "*May the Lord be with you*" from the early Christian faith, but Lucas did not desire for this film to be Christian in nature. Instead, he watered it down to be a generic tale of faith that is precisely what we find with the ecumenical movement and modernization of

Christianity. Father Seraphim Rose warned about this exact message in *Orthodoxy and the Religion of the Future* where he describes a future in which Christianity is watered down to the point of extinction. Indeed, George Lucas said that he wanted to *"awaken a certain kind of spirituality"* with the Force, and that it was *"distill[ed from] the essence of all religions."* [19]

George Lucas described his desire to lure the youth into his way of thinking which appears to be a generalized idea of religion:

There was no modern mythology to give kids a sense of values, to give them a strong mythological fantasy life,' he said later. 'Westerns were the last of that genre for Americans. Nothing was being done for young people that has real psychological underpinnings and was aimed at intelligent beings.' But in fact Lucas had no such intentions at the outset. If anything, the whole idea of religion was alien to him. He had gone to church as a boy, and even attended Catholic mass a few times at USC, but the last time he'd been in church was to be married. He was no mystic – he knew what a Chevy or an Arriflex would do, but a soul ...? [17]

Lucas wanted to find a path for everyone to walk that satisfied all religious beliefs, but Fr. Seraphim Rose warned that this kind of attitude was the chief heresy of the 20th century and it is preparing us for a world that appears Christian but is anti-Christian in nature and centered upon pagan experiences. [20]

Lucas was indeed planning to create a faith based on satisfaction of *all* faiths, as is described in his biography:

Here was a religion that, like Scientology, claimed to supersede every creed, every philosophy, every human aspiration – not, like L. Ron Hub-bard's synthetic creed, by illuminating their fallacies with the white light of science, but by subsuming all existing faiths. The Force was a belief roomy enough for Christianity, Buddhism and Islam to nestle in its ample folds. Tongue in cheek, Coppola would suggest to Lucas that he launch a religion based on Star Wars, and settle down like Hubbard to bask in his godhood. Once Skywalker Ranch was built, Lucas invited Joseph Campbell to lecture there, impressing John Williams, for one: 'Until [Campbell] told us what Star Wars meant – started talking about collective memory and cross-cultural shared history – the things that rattle around in our brains and predate language, the real resonance of how the whole thing can be explained – we regarded it as a Saturday-morning space movie.' [17]

How curious is it that L. Ron Hubbard (founder of the Church of Scientology) once made a statement that supported the theories of this book you are reading about the connections of the occult with science fiction entertainment:

"Science Fiction, particularly in its Golden Age, had a mission. To get man to the stars." [21]

The fact of the matter is that the characters of *Star Wars* are all experiencing the mysteries of pagan or eastern religious powers. Gary Kurtz partially inspired the concept of the Force with his studies into Buddhism and comparative religions:

'Comparative Religion is one of the things I studied in university,' says Kurtz. 'I also studied the Buddhist and Hindu sects, and studied Zen and Tibetan Buddhism, and also Native American spirituality; shamanistic methods and so on. I got out a lot of my old books, and we talked about it. If you trace back most religious thought to the teachings of the great prophets, whether Judeo-Christian tradition, or Muslim, or even Hindu or Buddhist, you start to see lots of similarities. The core philosophies are very very similar. The most obvious one is the Buddhist tradition about karma – the karmic action

35

that comes out of cause and effect. So the Force is an
amalgamation of lots of different things. [17]

If this sounds familiar, perhaps it's due to Aleister
Crowley's attempts to create a new, universal religion in
which the practices of Buddhism and Hinduism are
combined with Western Esotericism, witchcraft, and
ceremonial magick in order for the practitioner to find
god on his own while destroying Christianity in the
process. Witchcraft employs this exact thought process
when describing their beliefs in a grand creator:

To outsiders, it seems that this religion typically
worships a god and goddess, but they also believe in the idea of
an impersonal force that exists in our world. They believe that
"The All"; a female spirit, created a male spirit that provide the
"two halves of the whole"- a duality concept similar to yin and
yang and also the light and dark sides of the Force. This dual
sided energy birthed the entire universe. In fact, practitioners
are asked to call upon ancient deities who exist on the different
ends of the light and dark spectrum- from the wisdom of Athena
to the darkness of the underworld with Hecate. [22]

In fact, if you study the alleged members of the
Illuminati, you'll find that Aldous Huxley's name comes
up with the Fabian Society and the same ideals of
liberalizing the world. In a book called *The Star Wars*
Heresies: Interpreting the Themes, Symbols, and Philosophies
of Episode I, II, and III, it is quite curious that Huxley's
name should show up:

It also reminds me of what the British writer and
thinker Aldous Huxley called the "perennial philosophy." In it,
he identified a common thread running through nearly all
religious traditions. This thread followed that there was a vast
Ground of Being shared by all; that it is both transcendent and
immanent; and that the purpose of existence is to know, love,
and finally become one with this Ground. Huxley defined this

as the "Minimum Working Hypothesis," and the Force clearly fills this role in that galaxy far, far away. [18]

It should also be noted that *Episode VII* introduces us to the character in the First Order named General Armitage Hux; which is quite possibly a veiled reference to Aldous Huxley ('A'rmitage='A'ldous, 'Hux'='Hux'ley). This character was played by Domhnall Gleason who also played the roles of William Beasley in the *Harry Potter* series as well as a main character in *Ex Machina*- a film that shows us the dangers of progressing down the path of technology and the self-awareness of Artificial Intelligence (*Ex Machina* also had the *2nd* main character played by Oscar Isaac who plays Poe in *Episode VII*).

The Force was also described as an energy locked into what Gary Kurtz called Kaibur Crystals- a concept derived from Kurtz' time as a student of comparative religions. [23] This, of course is an occult belief that there exists a hidden mystical energy in our world that can be tapped into by the practitioner. Occultists believe in the hidden healing powers of crystals (and given its popularity- those that are not "occultists" also use them). LDS founder Joseph Smith used divining rods' hidden energy to hunt for treasure before using seer stones to garner visions used to write the Book of Mormon. Occult magicians believe that stones inherit special powers which are taken from this ethereal world spirit, as is described in Francis Barrett's 1801 *The Magus*, Chapter VIII. [24]

The central argument I'm presenting here is that the Force of *Star Wars* is merely an admiration for days of old when pagan beliefs dominated the world. Sacred stones and amulets similar to the Kaibur Crystal from which the Force emanates were used by pagans from the time of ancient Egypt and are even described in the Bible.

For example, in Exodus 7:10-12 we hear of the pagan mystery schools and the Egyptian magicians proving the power of the occult:

> *10 And Moses and Aaron went in unto Pharaoh, and they did so as the Lord had commanded: and Aaron cast down his rod before Pharaoh, and before his servants, and it became a serpent.*
>
> *11 Then Pharaoh also called the wise men and the sorcerers: now the magicians of Egypt, they also did in like manner with their enchantments.*
>
> *12 For they cast down every man his rod, and they became serpents: but Aaron's rod swallowed up their rods.* [25]

After years of researching the "Illuminati," it seems that there is a common thread that leads back to the pagan cradle of civilization and the mystery schools that went underground from the days of ancient Egypt. This occult knowledge has been handed down over the ages to those initiates deemed worthy to hear the esoteric ideas and philosophies, leaving others to hypothesize what the true teachings were.

Joseph Campbell's theory was that stories were to be poetry that inspired its viewers to feel inspired through the playing out of struggles that were actually internal. The symbols and archetypes were known by all who watched as a form of making contact with the collective unconscious. If the theories of Joseph Campbell are correct, then I believe George Lucas is under the same spell as many others that manufacture our entertainment. There is no doubt that Lucas, at minimum, briefly understood Campbell's theories (his biography claims that he listened to extracts on audio tapes in his car). [17]

One concept that continually resurfaces is that of the global consciousness. We witness this with the *Star*

Wars' Force because it claims that there lies an energy field all around us. This is the same concept as that of the global consciousness or Huxley's "perennial philosophy." It is the idea that there lies one single, universal truth from which all religions are based. We find this often times in New Age thought because Helena Blavatsky's Theosophy started the notion of this "ancient wisdom" that has been "kept from the masses" for many years. You'll see it referred to in *The Secret* which even shows us the emerald tablets of Thoth (a book allegedly written by Hermes Trismegistus or the Egyptian god of magic: Thoth). The New Agers participate in a similar line of thinking as Theosophists, ceremonial magicians, and occultists that seek to unify all forms of thought into one state of being.

Joseph Campbell spoke about this and I believe George Lucas contributed to this scheme of "evolution of consciousness" in which they slowly influence the masses to subscribe to this line of thinking:

When we turn now, with this image in mind, to consider the
numerous strange rituals that have been reported from the primitive
tribes and great civilizations of the past, it becomes apparent
that the purpose and actual effect of these was to conduct
people across those difficult thresholds of transformation that
demand a change in the patterns not only of conscious but
also of unconscious life. The so-called rites of passage, which
occupy such a prominent place in the life of a primitive society
(ceremonials of birth, naming, puberty, marriage, burial, etc.),

are distinguished by formal, and usually very severe, exercises of
severance, whereby the mind is radically cut away from the attitudes,
attachments, and life patterns of the stage being left behind. [8]

Campbell's ideas are echoed by George Lucas and other thought leaders in entertainment, as they seek to influence us to believe in the idea that there is an impersonal god, or field of energy. The ultimate end game is the destruction of Christianity and the advent of a new global religion.

Occultist Alice Bailey (a former Theosophist) spoke about this goal in *Problems of Humanity,* which she channeled from an ancient spirit guide named Djwal Khul:

"The day is dawning when all religions will be regarded as emanating from one great spiritual source; all will be seen as unitedly providing the one root out of which the universal world religion will inevitably emerge. Then there will be neither Christian nor heathen, neither Jew nor Gentile, but simply one great body of believers, gathered out of all the current religions. They will accept the same truths, not as theological concepts but as essential to spiritual living; they will stand together on the same platform of brotherhood and of human relations; they will recognize divine sonship and will seek unitedly to cooperate with the divine Plan ... Such a world religion is no idle dream but something which is definitely forming today." [26]

Alice Bailey's works were published through "The Lucis Trust" which was originally called "Lucifer Publishing Company" in honor of Lucifer. How interesting is it that we can once again point out the irony in George "Lucas."

Bailey believed that the disembodied spirit of Djwal Khul also inspired Helena Blavatsky's *The Secret Doctrine*. If you look at Blavatsky's *Isis Unveiled* you'll also see more talk on the strategic plan to destroy religion and introduce a global consciousness "force":

> *Our work, then, is a plea for the recognition of the Hermetic Philosophy, the anciently universal Wisdom-Religion, as the only possible key to the Absolute in science and theology.*
>
> *Be this as it may, the religion of the ancients is the religion of the future. A few centuries more, and there will linger no sectarian beliefs in either of the great religions of humanity. Brahmanism and Buddhism, Christianity and Mahometanism will all disappear before the mighty rush of facts.* [27]

We could keep going through examples, but the point I'm trying to make is that the generalized cosmic nature of the Force is comparable to the New Age's idea of an impersonal god that is an energy field. The occultists like this idea because it means there is no concept of good and evil; only connection or disconnection to the source energy. In this belief system, there are no "sins" and everyone can pursue their own Will at any and all costs.

We know that Joseph Campbell's work influenced Lucas and Kurtz with the hero's journey and the monomyth forming the backbone of the *Star Wars* story (Lucas referred to Campbell as a "person of magic"). How curious is it that Campbell's influence was a man named Adolf Bastian who *also* argued for a theory called the "psychic unity of mankind?" This theory hypothesized that all human beings share the same psychology and cognition- a unified field of energy.

Bastian's work in *Elementargedanken* supported Carl Jung's idea of archetypes which we see plenty of in *Star Wars...*

Chapter 3
Archetypes and the Hero's Journey

A key tenet of the conspiracy theory that one repeatedly stumbles upon is that of symbolism. Prominent psychoanalysts like Carl Jung said that *"symbols gave purpose to man"* and that is for good reason. In the past 50+ years we've been inundated with occult symbols and messages in seemingly innocuous events like the MTV Video Music Awards, Super Bowl Halftime Shows, and various other high profile rituals.

The theory behind these symbols is that the occultists are using them to speak to us on the subconscious level. The ancient cultures knew that symbols held power and were able to convey thoughts and messages, which is why they are used in occult practices, rituals and ceremonies.

For example, in ceremonial magick, the practitioner would draw a circle and triangle such that the demon spirit they conjure would appear inside of the triangle and be confined within it. Some claim that Beyoncé and Jay-Z are utilizing the triangle for similar nefarious purposes, but that is a topic for another time (for more see *SACRIFICE: MAGIC BEHIND THE MIC*).

Another great illustration of the theory was one that I learned about from a guest on my podcast that goes by the name of Dovakhiim. She suggested that all one needs to do is watch the 1980s film *The Golden Child* with Eddie Murphy to see why the occultists are obsessed with symbols. Just like in the film, they trap the Golden Child inside of a cage which is covered with various symbols. The symbols are believed to block his positive energy (the boy is believed to be a Tibetan mystic capable of super human feats; just like Helena Blavatsky's beliefs).

We see various symbols utilized by the Illuminati to demonstrate different beliefs. For example, the Mano Cornuto hand most associate with the rock 'n' roll devil horns, is said to represent the belief in an all-powerful deity known as Moloch (who has horns on his head). This deity was the one that many Canaanites sacrificed their children to in the Bible, which is part of the pagan complex that God set about to rid the world of.

Another symbol one often sees is that of the All Seeing Eye. This is believed to represent different ideas; one of which is that of the Freemason Grand Creator. Others say it represents the Watchers; the angels that came to watch over the humans until they began to lust and procreate with the women and made the race known as the Nephilim. These giants were considered an abomination so God sent the great deluge to wipe them out, but the occultists revere them through the usage of the All Seeing Eye symbol.

Another idea with the All Seeing Eye is that it represents the pineal gland. The serpent in the Garden of Eden promised Adam and Eve the knowledge which corresponds to the "opening of the eye;" a reference to the pineal gland. Many new agers and occultists believe in the concept of opening up the pineal gland (whether it be through chakra point activation or otherwise), in order to open the doors of perception to another realm. The history of the occult claims that we used to all have active pineal glands which allowed us to interact with the deities, but over time we evolved and the pineal gland became less pronounced. [28]

45

We see the symbol of the All Seeing Eye multiple times from *Star Wars*. On the movie posters for *Episode IV* and *Episode VII* they are prominently juxtaposed with the light crossing over the All Seeing Eye; suggesting the illumination of the characters into the ways of Luciferian doctrine.

Of course the list of symbols goes on much further; including Saturn cubes, twin pillars, bathtubs, and alchemy. The point is hidden in a coded language meant to speak to the viewer on the subconscious level. The Illuminati believe that they can saturate our reality with the symbols and it will manifest a new way of thinking. They are practicing what it takes to create the world in their image according to *their* will.

The symbols are comparable to the idea of the archetype in that it is a part of the collective unconscious. What that means is that we all have an understanding of a universal concept. Plato postulated that they were mental forms imprinted on the human soul. Carl Jung referred to these as archaic remnants, seeds of consciousness, or "primordial images" which became known as the "Jungian Archetypes." We see various Jungian Archetypes as events or actual figures. Either way, we can relate to them because we have an instinctual knowledge buried deep in our subconscious. That is why marketing typically uses a particular event or character because they realize that we can identify the situation quickly since it is already "learned knowledge."

Some archetype events include: birth, death, separation from parents, marriage, and unionizing opposites (this one is utilized often with the concepts of duality). Some archetype figures include that of the mother, father, child, devil, god, wise old man, joker, trickster, and the hero. [29]

The most popular characters from *Star Wars* fit the molds nicely:

Luke Skywalker- The Initiate who turns into The Hero (who separates from his parents)
Obi-Wan Kenobi- Wise Old Man
Darth Vader- The Devil
Han Solo- The Rebel

From these archetypes, we can build a story based upon Joseph Campbell's monomyth; or the hero's journey. The history of this train of thought was brought about from Campbell's studies when he compared all of the myths, fantasies, and stories from across many of the world's cultures and found that they typically followed a single pattern.

The basic pattern can be broken down into three parts. First, the subject is separated from the world they once knew. Next they are initiated into a new world where the hero is challenged in novel and typically dangerous ways. During this process they discover something different about themselves or the world they live in (typically through synchronistic guidance in the right direction). In this sense they are reborn, or alchemically transformed. Finally, they return to the world as a new evolved being and considered the crowned conqueror, or in terms of alchemy, the rising phoenix.

We can compare this to the concept of duality and even in the *Star Wars* realm of using the Force. One must traverse the darkness before finding the light. In terms of Jungian speak, this is the idea of exploring the darkest inner recesses of one's mind and finding the shadow self. It is a concept well represented in the iconic image of Luke Skywalker on Tatooine staring into the light and dark suns.

Campbell's ideas have been alleged to influence Lucas and Kurtz' story of *Star Wars*, and it definitely appears that it has been utilized in various other films and tales. What I find most interesting about Campbell is that he coined the term "Follow your bliss" which comes from studies into Hinduism. The idea is that even if you don't know who, or what, you are (we're talking about the philosophical ideas presented by Rene Descartes), you can always know where your bliss resides. This thought process is the same as Aleister Crowley's "True Will" and Paulo Coelho's "Personal Legend" from *The Alchemist*.

We see this demonstrated in *Star Wars: A New Hope* as follows:

Step 1: The Ordinary World. This is demonstrated when they show Luke Skywalker toiling away at droids on the planet of Tatooine.

Step 2: Call to Adventure. Luke is instructed by R2D2's hidden message from Princess Leia to save the galaxy.

Step 3: Refusal of the Call. Luke has fear on leaving his home planet.

Step 4: Supernatural Aid. Luke meets Ben Kenobi who shows him the way of the Force.

Step 5: Crossing the First Threshold. Luke and Kenobi meet Han Solo at the Mos Eisley cantina, where they arrange for his assistance to leave the planet of Tatooine.

Step 6: Road of Trials. Luke is tested in the ways of the Force, all the while meeting friends and enemies in strange new places.

Step 7: The Belly of the Whale. This is when Luke finally makes it to the Death Star.

Step 8: Meeting of the Goddess. Luke and his allies traverse the Death Star, facing several obstacles in order to locate and save Princess Leia.

Step 9: Refusal of the Return. Luke rescues Princess Leia and they share the Death Star blueprint with the Rebel Alliance. Luke has completed his task, but decides to continue helping the Alliance.

Step 10: The Magic Flight. Luke and the Rebel Alliance attempt to destroy the Death Star.

Step 11: Apotheosis. Luke successfully harnesses the Force and destroys the Death Star.

Step 12: The Crossing of the Return Threshold. Luke returns to the "Ordinary World" with the successful destruction of the Empire's Death Star. The celebration proves that he has indeed created a new world (based upon following his bliss and his "True Will").

This is not the full, comprehensive sequence that Joseph Campbell details in *The Hero with a Thousand Faces*, but it is more of a basic understanding of how it plays out in *Episode IV*. For instance, one of the missing steps is Atonement with the Father, which doesn't happen until *Episode VI*. The concept fits Campbell's narrative beautifully:

> *The problem of the hero going to meet the father is to*
open
> *his soul beyond terror to such a degree that he **will** be*
ripe to
> *understand how the sickening and insane tragedies of*
this vast
> *and ruthless cosmos are completely validated in the*
majesty of
> *Being. The hero transcends life with its peculiar blind*
spot and
> *for a moment rises to a glimpse of the source. He*
beholds the
> *face of the father, understands —and the two are*
atoned.* [8]

There is also the idea of the mother goddess, which may be represented by Anakin Skywalker's mother (which is eventually satisfied when he takes up a mate through Padme, or Queen Amidala). These women represent the Mother Earth or Gaia archetype.

The purpose for these stories is that we *must* be presented with a tale of this journey, otherwise we will provide it to ourselves through some kind of underlying program from birth, as Campbell postulates:

> *Apparently, there is something*
> *in these initiatory images so necessary to the psyche that if they*
> *are not supplied from without, through myth and ritual, they*
> *will have to be announced again, through dream, from within —*
> *lest our energies should remain locked in a banal, long-outmoded*
> *toy-room, at the bottom of the sea.* [8]

Campbell's theory is that the path of the mythological hero is an adventure through alchemical processes. The steps are similar: separation, initiation, and rebirth as the rising phoenix. We see a tale like this with the legend of Prometheus (which is specifically cited by Campbell in his book). This Luciferian doctrine is that Prometheus ascended to the heavens and stole fire in order to bestow these gifts to all of mankind (referred to as "boons" by Campbell).

The initiation phase is when the initiate goes through the purification and all of their energy is focused on transcending reality and the dissolution of their former self, or ego. During this stage, the hero may come across various mentors- represented in *Star Wars* as Obi-Wan Kenobi, Han Solo, or Princess Leia. In fact, the goddess figure from Campbell's theory is one that is symbolic as the guiding force the hero must follow before achieving enlightenment, which is precisely what we find with Luke Skywalker's rescue of Princess Leia.

> *Woman, in the picture language of mythology, represents the*
> *totality of what can be known. The hero is the one who comes to*

know. As he progresses in the slow initiation which is life, the

form of the goddess undergoes for him a series of transfigurations:

she can never be greater than himself, though she can always

promise more than he is yet capable of comprehending. She lures, she guides, she bids him burst his fetters. And if he

can match her import, the two, the knower and the known, will

be released from every limitation. Woman is the guide to the

sublime acme of sensuous adventure. By deficient eyes she is

reduced to inferior states; by the evil eye of ignorance she is

spellbound to banality and ugliness. But she is redeemed by the

eyes of understanding. The hero who can take her as she is,

without undue commotion but with the kindness and assurance

she requires, is potentially the king, the incarnate god, of her

created world. [8]

Similarly, we find Queen Amidala as the reigning goddess of *Episodes I-III*. Her planet is named Naboo, quite possibly after Nabu- the god of wisdom in Babylonian hierarchy. We know that she has the ability to see into Anakin's inner persona when they have a rather telling conversation in *Episode II*:

Padme: *You had a nightmare again last night.*

Anakin: *Jedi don't have nightmares.*

Padme: *I heard you.*

51

Anakin: *I saw my mother. I saw her as clearly as I see you now. She's suffering, Padme. She is in pain. They're killing her! I know I'm disobeying my mandate to protect you, Senator. I know I will be punished and possibly thrown out of the Jedi Order, but I must go. I have to help her! I'm sorry, Padme. I don't have a choice.*

We can also explore another idea of Padme as the goddess that is revered by the Illuminati occultists of modern day when we see her as the horned deity in one of her many costumes; a point that didn't go unnoticed by the author of *Star Wars Heresies*:

The ornate costumes the shape-shifting Amidala wears likewise evoke the divine feminine, particularly the headdresses and hairstyles worn in her palace as well as in the Senate. "Some figures of Astarte have two horns emerging from her head," Anne Baring and Jules Cashford wrote, citing another Babylonian deity in their definitive The Myth of the Goddess, "linking her to Ishtar and to Isis-Hathor in Egypt, for both wore the horned headdress." Indeed, Queen Amidala's image would have looked in no way out of place had it been discovered carved on a bronze seal, or chiseled in a burial chamber, or cast as a marble statue thousands of years ago. [18]

There are a few ideas for the worship of the horned goddess by today's Illuminati members. We already considered the horned deity of Moloch, but there is also a more complex consideration. The idea is mentioned by Kenneth Grant in *Aleister Crowley and the Hidden God*, in which it is revealed that evoking this goddess in order to "fuse the X with the O" will summon a great beast from the Abyss; thereby bestowing Isis' blessings upon the practitioner. [30]

Another reason for Padme's inclusion in the story is to relate the character of Anakin to the viewer.

He shows us his sensitive side such that the viewer has more sympathy for him when he fully turns to the dark side in *Episode III* and becomes the embodiment of evil: Darth Vader. Anakin becomes the dark hero (or the "antihero") by the time the credits roll, leaving audiences confused as to how they view Darth Vader, something the media was able to pick up on:

> "*Despite the original trilogy laying all the seeds for this portrayal, audiences seemed somewhat taken aback by it when they finally witnessed it firsthand.*" [18]

This concept of the dark hero is a reiteration of the Prometheus tale; in that it is trying to garner sympathy from the masses to understand that not all evil is truly "evil." Again, it's a subtle Luciferian technique that we see from the likes of many pieces of entertainment today (examples include *Malificent*, *Dexter*, *Deadpool*, etc.).

Another consideration of the goddess idea is that of Campbell's chapter on the virgin birth. In *Episode I* we hear Anakin's mother, Shmi Skywalker, claim that there was no father involved in his birthing. Joseph Campbell explained the mother goddess as follows:

> *The world-generating spirit of the father passes into the manifold*
> *of earthly experience through a transforming medium—the*
> *mother of the world. She is a personification of the primal element*
> *named in the second verse of Genesis, where we read that*
> *"the spirit of God moved upon the face of the waters."*" [8]

Of course we find out that Anakin turns into Darth Vader, who eventually does come back from the dark side through the emotion of love for his family (which is ironically banned by the Jedi Knighthood), and proceeds to destroy the Sith and bring balance to the Force which requires the sacrifice of self. This ultimately cements Anakin-Vader as the chosen and true dark hero of the *Star Wars* tale.

Adoration for this dark hero character was proven in the 1980s when a child won a contest held by *National Geographic World Magazine* in which his drawing of Darth Vader was carved onto the Washington National Cathedral in Washington D.C.

I suppose it's appropriate for a Luciferian character to appear on a church, considering the multitude of other pagan statues in our great capital city which is based on Roman and Egyptian pagan architecture...

The idea that *Star Wars* is a production that speaks to us on a subconscious level is one of great interest. If nothing else, it appears that it has successfully "communicated" to more people than most all other tales, given the box office success of the films. It seems that the story from long ago and far away could indeed be a story recognizable to all of us, yet we're unable to put a finger on our familiarity to it. Deeply embedded into our subconscious may lie some alternative "true history" of our cosmos and mankind's attempt to reach out and make contact with other worlds and a hidden field of energy.

Could it be that George Lucas was able to channel some of the ideas of Carl Jung and Joseph Campbell in order to directly access the collective unconscious of the masses?

I believe it to be so and that is based on the unprecedented desire by the masses for anything and everything "*Star Wars*" related. From action figures to entire religions based on the Jedi-isms of the characters, it seems that there is no other film that has been able to connect with the masses on such a global scale. This only reinforces the concepts of symbolism having its purpose and powers over the human mind, and how those in entertainment have truly cracked the code to massive mind control…

Chapter 4
Break on Through to the Dark Side: Aleister Crowley, The Abyss, Da'at Vader, Duality & Reconciliation of Opposites

In terms of occult doctrine, there is an idea that a hidden realm exists. Practitioners believe that one can access and conquer this space if properly prepared. In terms of the occult and the Illuminati, this realm is referred to by many names. Some call it The Abyss, others call it the Mauve Zone, while followers of Kabbalism call it Da'at- the hidden zone on the Tree of Life.

This Hebrew mysticism term "Da'at" means "knowledge", and this "bridge between idea and reality" illustrates how one's thoughts can eventually become reality. This idea is echoed by occultists who believe the cosmos are connected to the individual (recall "As Above So Below" as the motto of Wicca). The occult magician believes they can make the universe reflect their inner thought through rituals and other practices; similar to Luke's mastery of the Force.

In Kabbalah, the ten sephirot on the Tree of Life represent the emanations of God from which all of reality was created. This could arguably be where

Crowley, Grant, Blavatsky, Gardner, and other prominent occultists derived their belief in the ability for the mind to create reality.

This one particular sephirot known as Da'at is different from the others in that it represents a hidden knowledge, which is why it is omitted from most illustrations of the Kabbalah Tree of Life. This empty region on the Tree of Life is referred to as The Abyss and Aleister Crowley was particularly interested in the characteristics it possessed. He expressed his interest in *Little Essays Towards Truth* where he discussed Kabbalah as it pertains to his Thelema religion:

Beyond it stretches what is called The Abyss. This doctrine is extremely difficult to explain; but it corresponds more or less to the gap in thought between the Real, which is ideal, and the Unreal, which is actual. In the Abyss all things exist, indeed, at least in posse, but are without any possible meaning; for they lack the substratum of spiritual Reality. They are appearances without Law. They are thus Insane Delusions. [31]

Crowley went further to express the ideas that crossing this Abyss is a dangerous undertaking, from which one could lose their mind if not properly prepared. However, if one successfully traversed The Abyss, they would become a Master of the Temple in his A.A. Silver Star faith which indicates this high ranking individual has gained understanding of the universe.

What is interesting here is that there is also a belief in an *inverted* realm of the Tree of Life in which the sephirot each have representations of evil forces (an idea similar to the one we saw in the Netflix series *Stranger Things*). This inverted realm contains fallen angels which are referred to as the Qlippoth (also known as the realm of the damaged gods).

Freeman Fly and Jamie Hanshaw's *Weird Stuff: Operation Culture Creation* explained where I'm going with this precise train of thought as it applies to *Star Wars*:

> *In Star Wars: Revenge of the Sith, the Emperor Palpatine executes Order 66 or Operation: Knight Fall. These were orders that clone troopers were trained to obey without hesitation. It was the formal beginning of the great Jedi purge and Order 66 signified the rise of the great galactic empire. In Kabbalistic magic, the Qlipoth, or Fallen Angels, are represented by the number 66 or VV.* [11]

The principle here is that one must go into the darkest realm possible in order to come back as a newly reborn initiate in the ways of the occult. In terms of Campbell's Hero's Journey, this is the same as returning with the boons and the knowledge of one's super powers. While the Kabbalists believe that one can only truly know themselves once they understand their darkest shadow, Carl Jung believed this shadow mostly goes unnoticed by the individual and his or her ego. Jung said that symbols are used to speak to this subconscious realm where the creativity of mankind resides.

Carl Jung and Friedrich Nietzsche believed that reaching into the darkness of the inner shadow was necessary in order for one to individuate and become more true to themselves. The person must go past the persona mask they put on for the world, as well as the ego, to finally confront their inner shadow. This is comparable to Crowley's belief in full dissolution of the ego before confronting the guardian of The Abyss: Choronzon.

Alan Watts compared this process to the manure required to grow a rose and H.P. Lovecraft referred to it as the place where the Beast resides, from which the impulses and desires of man emanate.

Peter Levenda's *The Dark Lord: H.P. Lovecraft, Kenneth Grant, and the Typhonian Tradition in Magic* reveals how the Kabbalah Tree of Life and other antinomian systems authorize the exploration of the divine *and* the demonic. In the two Keys of Solomon of the Golden Dawn they have a "Greater Key" which deals with angels and planetary magic as well as the "Lesser Key" or "Goetia" which is the summoning of demons. [32]

In *Star Wars* we have a light and dark side of the Force- arguably a similar concept as the Greater and Lesser Keys of Solomon since both put you in contact with spirits from the corresponding side (an example is when we see Kylo Ren calling upon Darth Vader in *Episode VII*, or Luke Skywalker with Obi-Wan Kenobi in *Episode VI*).

The light and dark concepts of duality is arguably the main take away of the *Star Wars* films. An example would be in *Episode I* when a young Anakin Skywalker shows Padme how he is building a droid (C3PO) which prominently has *only* its left eye lit up. After Anakin sees this error, he places the right eye into socket; forming the fully merged version with both left and right. Padme responds by telling him *"He's perfect."*

This could be a symbolic retelling of the Eye of Horus and the battle that took place between Set and Horus over the throne of their father; Osiris. Set removed Horus' left eye which was later restored by the magician Thoth (ironically a name very similar to the ice planet of Hoth in *Episode V*). The purpose of the tale could be analogous to *Star Wars* in that we learn that Anakin is a magician of sorts with a natural ability to tap into the power of the universe; just like the ceremonial magicians believe they can do. He is perfected only when he harnesses the full spectrum and both sides of duality.

Interestingly enough, we see this concept of duality echoed by many of the aforementioned occultists as well as non-occultists. We see it through symbolism that displays the two colors of black and white which represent the absence and presence of all colors. A familiar symbol is that of the yin and yang which demonstrates that both sides of the spectrum are to be found in all things. Philosophers often times believe the concept of duality was created by mankind in order to make sense and categorize things.

For instance, a modern use of duality is to define good and evil, which is used to dictate what is acceptable by societal standards and what is not. We even see this practice in terms of occultism when we learn of the right or left hand paths that one can take to attempt contact with the divine.

We also see it in terms of white or black magic; a concept detailed in Ph.D. Stephen Flowers *Lords of the Left Hand Path*:

In a precise sense, the distinction between white and black magic is simply that white magic is a psychological methodology for the promotion of union with the universe and pursuing aims in harmony with those of the universe, while black magic is such a methodology for the exercise of independence from the universe and pursuing self-oriented aims. Structurally, white magic has much in common with religion as defined above, while black magic is more purely magical in and of itself. This is why magic as a category of behavior is often condemned by orthodox religious systems. [33]

You'll notice that the black magic is referred to as the route for separating oneself from the universe and effectively "unplugging from the Matrix." This left hand path is for those that seek to be independent of humanity and society's rules in order to obtain personal gain. As I mentioned before, this is believed to be separation from the stream of consciousness; not "evil."

In terms of the *Star Wars* tale, the Dark Side is to be the path one takes to achieve condemned and unnatural abilities. Stephen Flowers points out that orthodox religious systems condemn this attitude and have labeled it as "evil." We also see how this rebellious nature is depicted as the archetype of the fallen angel: Lucifer.

Similar to the attributes of the left hand path black magician, Lucifer wanted mankind to be independent actors on their own, without the oppression from an authoritative figure (or so Luciferians believe). Lucifer was attempting to be independent and his rebellion caused him to be cast out of the Heavens which led him to become Satan. We see bits of this in *Episode III* when Anakin kills Count Dooku in front of the Emperor (Darth Sidius) and is consoled when Sidius tells him that revenge is only natural, which appeals to the animalistic side of mankind and is truly satanic at its core.

On the other hand, some believe that Lucifer is actually the entity of the light, with *his* opposition being the true evil and representative of the dark.

Either way, there is a focus to be had on the concept of duality with the light and dark sides of the Force. It seems obvious that the dark side corresponds to evil; until you consider some of the details of the plot that suggest it otherwise...

For instance, in *Episodes I* and *II* we are led to sympathize with Anakin as he tries to protect his family while failing to adhere to the Jedi Code which tells him he shouldn't even have a family. He believes Padme is going to die, and in an attempt to save her, he utilizes the dark side of the Force (which is why in *Episode II*, we hear that a Jedi Knight can't have attachment or possessions). We all know that he turns into Darth Vader which is used in *Episodes IV* and *V* to reiterate that he is "evil." When we watch *Episode VI* we are again left confused because Vader comes back to the light in order to destroy the Sith and save his son- Luke Skywalker.

So what are we to believe of Darth Vader and the duality of the Force?...

Consider that we are led to believe that Jedis are the powers of good (we are told they use the light side of the Force), as well as the idea that the Sith are the powers of evil (since they are the dark side). Anakin fails to obey the Jedi who tell him he shouldn't be married (which makes him the rebel, or Lucifer character). He listens to his emotions which guide him towards the dark side in order to protect the ones he loves. His character is sympathized by the viewer until he turns into Darth Vader (*Episode III*), at which point his original 1978 *first* impression (*Episode IV*) tells us he is evil.

To me, this is the portrayal of Lucifer as the evil one, no different than Darth Vader. When we see *Episode VI* and Darth Vader saving his son, we are left to assume he came back to the light side. However, it brings into question the ways of the Jedi Knights (the light side of the Force) since they said attachment to family members was forbidden. Anakin/Vader defied this rule and proved that he was capable of doing good while being in touch with the dark side. Anakin/Vader, therefore, is the misunderstood and fallen angel who shows us that there is no such thing as good or evil, light or dark. They are all the same in the *Star Wars* message.

If you look at this *Star Wars* tale differently you could see it as a tale of reconciling opposites. Good and evil are to be looked at as two sides to the same coin- both of which can be used by free agents to find their own path in reality. The practitioner is free to unite or separate from the divine since both paths are of no consequence. In this we see that *same message* because Anakin/Vader shows us the ability to be good- even when labeled as "evil."

63

Ken Ammi wrote about this blurring of good and evil in his *Star Wars* article title *"Everything I know about the occult, I learned from watching Star Wars"*:

There are also concepts of necromancy and ascended masters within the mythos as, for example, when Obi Wan Kenobi passes away, he can not only speak into Luke Skywalker's mind but appear to him as a type of specter. But not only can Kenobi, and those who have attained his level, speak to one's mind; he can manipulate the person into actually acting against their own wills. Jedi can, and do, take over other's minds to force them into a certain set of actions. In real life this would be considered black magick sorcery—and this is the supposed good guy Jedi doing it.

The Sith have a planet sized device called the Death Star and once the Jedi Rebels destroy it, Luke Skywalker see the manifestation of a, by then, deceased Jedi Master Obi Wan Kenobi, Jedi Master Yoda and Sith Lord Darth Vader. So, apparently, the Star Wars mythos is universalist; all are "saved" and thus, end up in the same place, the same realm of afterlife existence—although, the mythos may have played off of the idea of Vader repenting in the end and actually fighting a Sith Lord in order to save his son Luke Skywalker. [34]

The entire aim of the tale is that of reconciling opposites, which suggests that *Star Wars* has an occult flavor of Gnosticism. This early esoteric version of the Christian faith believes in the importance of merging good with evil. They believe that we are all connected and one being, similar to Pantheism, Panentheism and many of the New Age schools of thought we've already discussed.

Dr. Jeffrey Satinover wrote about this in *The Empty Self: C.G. Jung & the Gnostic Transformation of Modern Identity*:

"...the ultimate aim... of all Gnostic systems is a mystical vision of the union of good and evil." [35]

64

Monotheism is the belief in one God, meanwhile Gnostics, Carl Jung, Hinduism, New Age, and other occultists believe in monism- the claim that we are all one; and we, along with nature, *are* god. This includes good, evil, right, wrong, male, female, light and dark. Carl Jung studied this concept from the perspective of alchemy and attributed it to part of the individuation process to learn these things.

The practice of alchemy is one to be considered when viewing the Illuminati and the ways of the occult. In it, they seek a "Rebis" which is a term for the reconciled opposites- sometimes described as the union of male and female. In Robert Allen Bartlett's *Real Alchemy: A Primer of Practical Alchemy*, he describes one of the "mothers" of alchemy and her explanation of the same process:

*"Maria the Jewess, one of our mothers of alchemy, alluding to Hermes, elucidates the role of opposites in the act of creation when she says, "*Make the corporeal incorporeal and the incorporeal corporeal, join male and female and you shall have what you seek."" [36]

Stephen Flowers, Ph.D. explains this when he details Crowley's definition of "The Devil" as the God of any people that one personally dislikes. Crowley also claims that Satan was the true savior and *not* the enemy of man because he knew "good and evil" and taught initiation through sayings such as "Know Thyself!" The Devil is symbolized as the Baphomet because this is: *"the androgyne who is the hieroglyph of arcane perfection."* [33]

The idea of androgyny as a perfected being is demonstrated by alchemists as well; particularly when illustrating the Rebis when they show a body that is half woman and half male (just like the Baphomet- a male with breasts). This concept of magickal union is demonstrated when we see Aleister Crowley reference this same idea in *Confessions*:

"*[T]he true magick of Horus requires the passionate union of opposites.*" [37]

Without going *too* far into the deep end of the occult, the concept of the Baphomet is another illustration of this concept in practice through symbolism. The Baphomet symbol is the man with a goat head and female breasts- indicating he has indeed reconciled opposites and become an enlightened Rebis of alchemy. It's of no coincidence that the Church of Satan also utilizes this as their symbol, referring to it as the Sigil of Baphomet.

Flowers goes on to explain that Aleister Crowley himself was monistic (the same as Carl Jung- believing there is no true duality of good and evil and all things should be reconciled as one since "God" is everywhere and everything). The belief is that all opposites are unities in reality, and this is how Horus united with Set and the reason we have "*light and dark opposites within the same unity.*" [33]

Aleister Crowley believed that the magician should find a way to "destroy evil" by reconciling these opposites and he uses interesting language to do so:

"*The Magician should devise for himself a definite technique for destroying "evil." The essence of such practice will consist in training the mind and body to confront things which cause **fear, pain**, disgust, shame and the like. He must learn to endure them, then to become indifferent to them, then to analyse them until they give pleasure and instruction, and finally to appreciate them for their own sake, as aspects of Truth.*" [33]

I find it interesting that Crowley uses the same terms to describe "evil" as Yoda does to describe the dark side of the Force:

"Fear is the path to the dark side. Fear leads to anger. Anger leads to hate."

Yoda also described a similar method for reconciling the opposites of good and evil:

"Train yourself to let go of everything you fear to lose."

Recall that Crowley advised to confront fear and learn to endure it and become indifferent to it before eventually appreciating it...

Let's take a step back and see how this applies to *Star Wars*. The reconciliation of opposites is used to show that light and dark are both *one and the same* and indeed *not* different. The occultists believe that there is no such thing as good or evil, and that Christianity and other religions are responsible for this form of societal programming. Aleister Crowley sought to join good with evil and prove that they are both the same thing and all things are simply expressions of love and god:

"Let there be no difference . . . between any one thing and any other thing." –Aleister Crowley, *The Book of the Law* [38]

We are told about this concept of reconciling opposites when *Star Wars* constantly speaks about bringing "balance" to the Force. The show is not intended to obliterate evil, but rather bring it into the fold as a potential path of life. The light and dark sides of the Force are both still expressions of a universal energy but are truly only the same thing.

If destroying evil completely *was* the aim- it would *not* bring balance since the light side would be the

67

only one left in existence. It makes no sense to think destroying evil would bring balance to the Force since, by definition, there would need to be a dark and light side of equal magnitude for there to be a balance (which apparently already exists). Instead, they are showing us that the dark is the same as the light when we see Anakin become a practitioner of the dark side, yet is able to still love and be a part of the light side when in *Episode VI* he saves Luke Skywalker.

Both sides of the Force are "in balance" because there is no such thing as a good or evil side. It is only "the Force" and Anakin who successfully reconciled the opposites (he is the "chosen one" born through immaculate conception; proven in *Episode I* when his mother says there is no father and she doesn't know how it happened).

Darth Vader was the true hero the entire time- the dark, antihero that proves to the audience that bad really is good. Luke Skywalker is not intended to be a hero; he is merely one part of the hero since he is required to be a juxtaposition next to Darth Vader in order to demonstrate the occult principle of reconciliation of opposites.

The fact that Anakin is called the chosen one and is born through the immaculate conception only further proves that he is the "moon child" of Aleister Crowley's description in his novel called *"Moonchild."* It is a tale based on the beliefs of magick and the attempts to conceive a special chosen "moonchild" that will save humanity and improve its condition. Coincidentally, the story revolves around a battle between *white* and *black* magicians...

This is similar to the idea presented in a major influence and predecessor to *Star Wars* with Stanley Kubrick's *2001: A Space Odyssey*. This tale is described in my Kubrick film analysis, *KUBRICK'S CODE,* as a veiled lesson in alchemy where an alien race successfully births a moon child (called a "star child" in *2001*) in order to save humanity.

    Star Wars is a Luciferian tale inspired by hints of New Age, Gnosticism, Hinduism, Aleister Crowley, and occult teachings. They are telling us that the fallen angel is not truly "evil" and that the social construct of dualism with good and evil is merely an illusion.

Chapter 5
The Alien Agenda

The full scope of the Illuminati's agenda includes the plan to entice the masses to worship demons from the sky. They will do this by making us believe in the existence of extraterrestrials. We see the existence of E.T. life forms throughout *Star Wars* and it is part of the entertainment industry's push to nudge its followers in the direction they desire.

They are already indoctrinating many people in the ways of the Ancient Astronaut Theory on a show called *Ancient Aliens*. When you look at the history of this belief system you'll find that it didn't originate with Giorgio Tsoukalos or Erich von Daniken. Nor was it from Zecharia Sitchin's talk of the Illuminati and his interpretation of the Sumerian cuneiform script (which has been proven false- as documented by various scholars, including Michael Heiser, which was proven on December 21st, 2012 when Planet Nibiru did in fact not reveal itself or change the world as we know it). [39]

The roots of the Ancient Astronaut Theory go back to Konstantin Tsiolkovsky who influenced scientists like Wernher von Braun to get man to the stars in order to find our creators.

Besides the fact that Nibiru, aka Planet X, doesn't exist, and the fact that most of the *Ancient Aliens* theorists are not scholars, archeologists or anthropologists; people are still being influenced by the Ancient Astronaut craze (I've most certainly been guilty of falling under its spell in the past as well). Erich von Daniken started the Archaeology, Astronautics and SETI Research Association, but he is indeed not an astronaut nor an archeologist (he was alleged to be a hotelier who authored books on the side- worse yet he was allegedly arrested for fraud and embezzlement). [40]

The poster child for *Ancient Aliens* is the wild-haired Giorgio Tsoukalos, who does not have a degree in anthropology or archeology, but instead graduated in sports information and communication and then proceeded to become a bodybuilding promoter. [41]

David Childress refers to himself as a "rogue archeologist" who also stars on *Ancient Aliens*, but he did not graduate with a degree of any sort (technically he enrolled to do so but dropped out the next year). [42] Instead, he learned about New Age Lumerian theories from Richard Kieninger- a man who was alleged to have plagiarized content and kicked out of multiple groups for inappropriate relations with young women. [42]

I'm not saying the *Ancient Aliens* show isn't interesting, intriguing, or entertaining. I *am* saying that it is simply not factually accurate. I think it's great to open up minds to consider other ideas, but people are believing this alternate version of New Age theory as fact. If you look at who created this content, you'll see the connection I'm making with *Star Wars*: Prometheus Entertainment.

Yes, *Ancient Aliens* is another piece of the entertainment agenda to push Luciferian tales as reality to an unsuspecting population. *Star Wars* is also a tool being used since its popularity is off the charts and accessible to multiple generations of viewers.

For instance, when you consider the predictive programming of the *Star Wars* clone wars against the allegations that a real clone war is imminent; it seems that some of the reality and fiction lines are blurred.

A whistleblower named Donald Marshall claims to have been an Illuminati insider who witnessed many of the things we've come to understand about this secretive group. He said that they have cloning centers in which they replicate world leaders so they can meet in private; starting back in the 1940s. He also alleges that they eventually started experimenting with the cloning of celebrities and entertainers in order for them to "indulge their every fantasy." [43]

Marshall describes his experiences through his late night kidnappings from his room during his sleep (akin to the alien abduction phenomenon). He claims they use a top secret technology known as R.E.M. Driven Consciousness Transfer in order to transfer consciousness from the sleeping person to the clone (similar to that concepts shown to us in *Avatar*).

I realize that I just made an effort to debunk *Ancient Aliens* by proving the theorists have no basis in their field of study, and now I'm asking the reader to listen to the testimony of a man who claims to be a victim of an Illuminati experiment in cloning, but I give some clout to what Donald Marshall is saying because of one thing he describes in his narrative:

Marshall suggests you give your favorite songs another listen as he says that he "left a thousand clues in a thousand songs", such as in the 1983 breakthrough hit for British duo, the Eurythmics's Sweet Dreams (Are Made of This). The song achieved global success for the musical couple, topping charts all over the world, including the U.S. [43]

I fully believe that aspect of his story because I've been witnessing it through many years of researching the occult with music and film. It seems obvious that entertainment is the tool for pushing the agenda, especially considering America's fascination with pop culture, reality stars, and anything that will "unplug" us from reality. Francis Bacon once talked about how to instill an idea into the masses and he said it was much easier to demonstrate it through entertainment than to directly lecture them.

He was undoubtedly spot-on...

By the way- if you're curious as to Marshall's claim on the *Sweet Dreams* song, he is referencing these lyrics:

"Some of them want to use you, Some of them want to be used by you, Some of them want to abuse you, Some of them want to be abused by you."

He says that this is precisely what he witnesses at the cloning centers, where the Illuminati subject the clones of celebrities and entertainers in every evil way possible.

Let's entertain the theories of Donald Marshall and see how it relates to *Star Wars*...

He alludes to the fact that George Lucas showed us the Clone Wars in *Episodes II* and *III* along with the aliens known as the Kaminoan in the *Star Wars* Universe. Marshall claims these Kaminoan are in fact the exact depictions of a certain species of aliens he encounters in his experiences with the Illuminati. [44]

We learn that the grey aliens were the ones that genetically modified Jango Fett's offspring in order to create the Clone Army. This concept is very similar to the Ancient Astronaut Theory that believes mankind was aided in its evolution by the DNA manipulation from an alien race.

The Clone Wars were used to turn the Galactic Republic into the Galactic *Empire*- making the Sith Lord Republic Supreme Chancellor Palpatine the dictator, similar to Adolf Hitler's rise to power through emergency powers in Germany. [45] How interesting that we find the Hitler connection, since the Nazi party

74

was particularly interested in channeling aliens through the VRIL and THULE society...

The Nazi party allegedly conducted many mind control experiments of their own at the direction of Dr. Joseph Mengele, which coincides with some of the ideas presented in *Star Wars*. Not only do we have the mind controlled clones, but in *Episode VII* we find out from General Hux that his troops were "programmed from birth"- classic traumatic mind control, similar to what Cathy O'Brien went through in Project MONARCH.

Finishing the thought on the *Star Wars* Clone Wars; we find the final surge through the execution of Order 66. I previously discussed the Qlippoth and the 66 fallen angels that exist in the shadow realm on the Tree of Life, so it seems appropriate to find out that the Kaminoan (grey aliens) clone troops were instilled with the instructions of the "fallen angels" through Order 66 which resulted in the double cross of the Jedis in *Episode III*. Furthermore, we find out that depictions of the Kaminoan in *Star Wars* was "officially" based on the aliens from Spielberg's *Close Encounters of the Third Kind*. [46]

We also know that *Close Encounters of the Third Kind* was mentioned by the late Bill Cooper in his ground breaking book *Behold a Pale Horse*:

> *Project SIGMA and a new project, PLATO, through radio communications using the computer binary language, were able to arrange a landing that resulted in face-to-face contact with alien beings from another planet. This landing took place in the desert. The move,* Close Encounters of the Third Kind *is a fictionalized version of the actual events.* [47]

Bill Cooper prefaced that chapter with the disclaimer that he was exposed to secret documents while in Naval Intelligence between 1970 and 1973 and the material in the chapter was based on those findings. He often times expressed concern as to whether or not the documents were shown to him as disinformation or the real thing.

Upon even further digging, we can see other alien entities in the *Star Wars* Universe being named after the VRIL society, which is of importance because occultists seem to believe in this alien race as an authentic reality. In the extended *Star Wars* Universe, we find aliens with names like Eaden Vrill and Vril Vrakth. I believe that these may have been influenced by the rest of the *Star Wars* symbolism since they are apparently from the spirit of alien that Hitler and Blavatsky sought to make contact.

Blavatsky mentions a book called *The Coming Race* as well as the Vril multiple times in her books *Isis Unveiled* and *The Secret Doctrine*:

If the question is asked why Mr. Keely was not allowed to pass a certain limit, the answer is easy; because that which he has unconsciously discovered, is the terrible sidereal Force, known to, and named by the Atlanteans MASH-MAK, and by the Aryan Rishis in their Ashtar Vidya by a name that we do not like to give. It is the vril of Bulwer Lytton's "Coming Race," and of the coming races of our mankind. The name vril may be a fiction; the Force itself is a fact doubted as little in India as the existence itself of their Rishis, since it is mentioned in all the secret works. [48]

She believed the Vril to be an energy force that could help mankind to unlock his latent super powers. Adolf Hitler allegedly sought contact with this Vril force through the VRIL Society when he used spirit channelers like Maria Orsic to seek contact. Supposedly they were able to make contact and learned the secrets of travel through the flying saucers and experiments like Die Glocke (especially if you consider the sightings of Foo Fighters and bell shaped UFOs since then).

Hitler acknowledged the influence of a man named Dietrich Eckart in his book *Mein Kampf* when he stated:

"I should like to mention the name of a man who devoted his life to reawakening his and our people through his writing and his ideas and finally through positive action. I mean: Dietrich Eckart." [49]

Dietrich Eckart was affiliated with an esoteric occult group known as the Thule Society, who believed in a German Messiah who would return the country to its former glories. The Thule Society was conducting séances and communication with demonic entities in order to bring this incarnation of the Antichrist to fruition, and in a somewhat nefarious set of circumstances, we ended up with Adolf Hitler. [50]

Eckart claimed that Hitler had the power to communicate with spirits as well, which supports the idea that Hitler would pursue this line of thinking. Hitler and other Nazi occultists continued to channel information from alien entities and obtaining knowledge on practices such as *cloning an army of soldiers.* [50]

After the end of World War II, there proved to be a German-occult influence exported to the United States of America through Operation Paperclip when several German Nazi scientists got out of town and helped bring Nazi rocket technology to the United States of America.

Jack Parsons started the federally funded Jet Propulsions Laboratory in 1936, which eventually teamed up with Nazi scientist Wernher von Braun in 1954 before eventually being absorbed by NASA in 1958. Consider that the pioneers of space travel were occultists who sought to bring Aleister Crowley's work to the next generation, and there seems to be cause for concern.

For example, it's no secret that Jack Parsons was fond of Crowley, to the point that he claimed to be the heir in secession to Crowley and even called himself the Antichrist in 1949's *The Book of Antichrist* written by himself:

And thereafter I was taken within and saluted the Prince of that place, and thereafter things were done to me of which I may not write, and they told me, "It is not certain that you will survive, but if you survive you will attain your true will, and manifest the Antichrist.

And thereafter I returned and swore the Oath of the Abyss, having only the choice between madness, suicide, and that oath. But the Oath in no wise ameliorated that terror, and I continued in the madness and horror of the abyss for a season. But of this no more. But having passed the ordeal of 40 days I took the oath of a Magister Templi, even the Oath of Antichrist before Frater 132, the Unknown God.

And thus was I Antichrist loosed in the world; and to this I am pledged, that the work of the Beast 666 shall be fulfilled, and the way for the coming of BABALON be made open and I shall not cease or rest until these things are accomplished. And to this end I have issued this my Manifesto. [51]

We see Parsons speaking about taking the Oath of the Abyss, indicating he had familiarity with the Qlippoth and the "Order 66" fallen angels. He also proceeds to talk about taking an oath to destroy the *"lying hypocrisy of Christianity."* [51]

The idea that NASA may have occult intentions seems preposterous on the surface, but theorists like Serge Monast have asserted that is in fact what is going on. He claims there exists a "Project Blue Beam" that NASA utilizes in order to push us into a New Age belief system and a false return of Christ. He details a four step plan to implement this new world order, with the first step being the "breakdown of all archaeological knowledge" where fake earthquakes will reveal discoveries and artifacts that disprove all religious doctrines.

The second step will have a "space show" that depicts the coming of an Antichrist.

Steps three and four detail the telepathic communication of the entity with its followers as well as faked alien invasions and the people begging the governments of the world to come together and create a One World Order. [52]

What is alarming about Monast's claims from the 1990s is the advent of the *Ancient Aliens* show which is in fact "breaking down archaeological knowledge." Also consider that NASA's Chief Scientist said there are *"strong indications of life beyond Earth"* in 2016. She also warned:

"I think we're going to have strong indications of life beyond Earth within a decade. I think we're going to have definitive evidence within 20 to 30 years." [53]

NASA cites recent discoveries that suggest our own solar system could have environments to support life. Alarmingly enough, they cite the potential for liquid water on the Jupiter moon of Europa which they are slotted to launch for investigation in 2022 for the purpose of finding alien life. [54]

The reason I say this is alarming is because Arthur C. Clarke's novels from the *2001: A Space Odyssey* series (followed by the novels *2010: Odyssey Two*, *2061: Odyssey Three*, and *3001: The Final Odyssey*) reveal that there is an extraterrestrial race monitoring and seeding lifeforms through the process of evolution. These alien beings have had their consciousness transferred into pure energy in the attempts to become immortal travelers of the cosmos (recall Donald Marshall's statement about the transferring of consciousness).

The alien race instructs the humans to avoid one place in the entire cosmos: Europa; which is precisely where we are headed in 2022 in order to look for alien life.

In *2010: Odyssey Two* it is revealed that the planet Jupiter is blown up by the alien monoliths in order for it to become a sun named "Lucifer" which melts the ice on Europa (*as a side note, it appears that Han Solo is frozen inside of what looks like a monolith in *Episode V*). This initiates the sequence of life that is being monitored by the alien beings which the humans are instructed *not* to investigate.

Ultimately- Arthur C. Clarke's *2001* books are more Luciferian doctrine embedded with programming of ancient astronaut theory.

It seems to me that the Illuminati use entertainment to demonstrate concepts; whether it be predictive programming in order for our minds to more readily accept this "new truth," or fear tactics used to avoid certain schools of thought. The fact that NASA, *Ancient Aliens*, and *Star Wars* are showing the same Luciferian doctrine of consciousness transfer along with ancient astronaut theory is one we should consider when looking at the overall theme of the big agenda.

Chapter 6
Conclusion: Aeon of The Force

The idea that *Star Wars* is a veiled attempt at swaying the minds of the masses is not one that will be accepted easily. The fact that so many people have been life-long fans of the symbolism, character archetypes and tales from the *Star Wars* Universe is quite telling in the argument that entertainment wields great power. Indeed, the power of the Force is undeniable, but we must ask ourselves who, or *what*, is behind this agenda?

Father Seraphim Rose believed that science fiction entertainment is a coordinated attempt by the dark forces of Satan and those that worship him. Fr Rose claimed that the concept of a universal consciousness was merely one (of many) paths that could be taken to destroy Christianity once and for all. Watering down religion to an attitude of vague "spirituality" is precisely what Satan *may* be doing in order to dilute the true teachings of Christ and usher in this new age of a universal world religion.

The 1960s brought in the Age of Aquarius attitude which would eventually give way to the worship of individuality in the current age. These New Age ideals were carried through to modern times in which many are practicing yoga and meditation as a lifestyle when in reality these were practices intended to put one in contact with fallen spirits. We see this in *Episode III* when Yoda tells Obi-Wan Kenobi about the path to immortality and how to communicate with him is through channeling of his disembodied spirit.

George Lucas himself alluded to this technique when asked at a 1981 *Revenge of the Jedi* conference when he compared the Force directly to yoga:

> **Kasdan:** The Force was available to anyone who could hook into it?
> **Lucas:** Yes, everybody can do it.
> **Kasdan:** Not just the Jedi?
> **Lucas:** It's just the Jedi who take the time to do it.
> **Marquand:** They use it as a technique.
> **Lucas:** Like yoga. If you want to take the time to do it, you can do it; but the ones that really want to do it are the ones who are into that kind of thing. Also like karate. Also another misconception is that Yoda teaches Jedi, but he is like a guru; he doesn't go out and fight anybody. [55]

Star Wars echoes the ideas of "Law of Attraction" when it said that focus determines reality- a concept delivered by the New Age body of work called *The Secret*.

Many are looking for a religion that fits *their* lifestyle, because Aleister Crowley's Aeon of Horus and the age of the "crowned and conquering child" pursuing their own "Will" is truly coming to fruition. This idea of finding God from within ourselves and connecting to this "universal Force" on our own is truly a Gnostic and Freemason ideal. [20]

We see Anakin demonstrating this multiple times. His over-confidence in himself is shown when he questions his Jedi elders throughout the series. In *Episode II* he uses the Force and telekinesis to move a pear, and states that Obi-Wan Kenobi would be very upset if he were to be caught doing it. All of these suggest his desire to pursue his own Will and not live according to the traditional standards of those before him.

The reality is that the true teachings of Christianity are to do *God's* Will. It's right there in the Lord's Prayer when He says: "...*Thy Will be done on Earth as it is in Heaven.*" I believe this is because God knows the struggles that come with the Satanic trappings of the material world, and how easily we can fall into a prideful state of self-worship.

Even if you don't want to consider the Christian aspects of all this (I acknowledge that not everyone who reads my books is a Christian or even religious at all); one should see the push for the destruction of Christianity as a key goal of this "Illuminati" agenda. It appears that a multi-faceted approach is being used to appeal to *anything* that diverts people away from the Christian faith.

For instance, in *Star Wars* we see the recurrent message of the evolved being having super powers, which suggests that man can somehow become "God" through education of secret doctrines and evolution, which also contributes to inflating the ego and appealing to our pride. We see Luke Skywalker evolve through continuous efforts to harness powers of the Force in an attempt to become a fully transformed initiate of Alchemy. The Hindus believe that God is man, who can become divine by realizing the divine (e.g. The Force). [20]

When you consider the traits found across most *all* sci-fi tales, you'll begin to see a pattern. They show us a future that is devoid of Christianity, which is replaced by a pagan worship of multiple gods or a cosmic consciousness. We can see the comparison of the Force to the older pagan religions in *Episode IV* when Darth Vader chokes a man after he mocks the Force and refers

84

to it as "old religion and sorcery" because that is indeed what it is; an ancient belief in the power of magick.

We also see an evolved and improved form of mankind which has super powers or integrated technology which creates the next revolution of humanity as the transhuman; effectively blurring magick with reality in a future that is obsessed with occult ideals. The fact that comic book super hero and sci-fi tales are the most popular films is quite telling of our culture's fascination with a potential future.

We see these concepts in *Star Wars* when we hear of midi-chlorians being in the people that have "greater" contact with the Force. We are also subjected to depictions of sorcerers and divination when Luke channels the fallen spirits of Jedi Masters, or in *Episode VI* when Yoda and Luke search for Han Solo and Princess Leia. Also, Darth Vader demonstrates his ability to levitate as a form of siddhi or enlightenment, akin to the claims of many Hindu gurus.

All of these techniques and practices were supposedly utilized by ancient super-cultures such as those of Atlantis, Lemuria, or other "golden age" societies that practiced magick and possessed great supernatural powers. These were cultures from long ago and far away- quite similar to the universe of *Star Wars*.

Helena Blavatsky's Theosophical Society talked about contacting these cultures and claimed they were channeling Integrated Ascended Masters from the Ashtar Command in order to learn more about the perfected form that mankind is capable of achieving. [56] A belief within this same realm was that there was a concentrated stream of spiritual energy emanating from a perfected source that was called a "Ray;" which begs the question of Rey's purpose in *Episode VII* since she is able to tap into *her* latent super human powers of the Force.

The idea of an evolved form of man that was seeded from extraterrestrial visitors seems to go hand in hand with the belief in white supremacy, especially since Adolf Hitler apparently subscribed to as least *some* of the Theosophical ideals. Blavatsky referred to this "superior" form as a "root race" in *The Secret Doctrine*- a book that Hitler was alleged to possess which inspired his pursuit of his form of the Aryan super-man (referred to by Blavatsky as the Fifth Root Race):

> *The first root-race, i.e., the first "men" on earth (irrespective of form) were the progeny of the "celestial men," called rightly in Indian philosophy the "Lunar Ancestors" or the Pitris, of which there are seven classes or Hierarchies.* [48]

When *Episode VII* was released in 2015, many claimed there were racial undertones. Some claimed that the lack of white men in the film pushed forward an anti-white agenda (made famous by the #BoycottStarWarsVII hashtag movement), while others claimed the actual role of a black man (Finn) was intended to show a slave who *needed* the white people to save him from his role of servitude to the First Order. The support for that idea is in Finn's name which is only given to him after he is freed from his slavery as FN-2187 (akin to the practice of slavery when the slave master renamed the slave in order to further separate them from their home). To further provoke this theory, the posters released in China for the film showed Finn's image greatly reduced and placed into the background.

While some claim that J.J. Abrams is pushing the *genocide* of white men due to the casting of non-whites in *Episode VII* (citing that he is a Jewish director), I believe there is a desire to pursue what the occultists refer to as the "Great White Brotherhood." We'll discuss why this *isn't* racist soon, but first let's take a quick look at it.

Karl von Eckartshausen was a German occultist-mystic from the mid-1700s that was in the actual Bavarian Illuminati and wrote *The Cloud Upon the Sanctuary* which inspired Aleister Crowley's A.A. order

[57] when von Eckartshausen referred to this group of "enlightened" extraterrestrials as the "community of light":

This community of light has been called from all time the invisible celestial Church, or the most ancient of all communities. [58]

These Ascended Masters are believed to be a more evolved form of mankind that have mastered the lessons of this world and turned into a superior god-form (similar to the progression of *2001: A Space Odyssey's* David Bowman as he turns into Halman- the evolved transhuman form of David Bowman and HAL9000 that we learn of in *3001: The Final Odyssey*).

All of these occultists are referring to this group of super-humans that are also called the Great White Brotherhood. When they use the term "white" they are referring to the practice of white magick; or the light side of the Force if we consider *Star Wars*.

An interesting parallel between Nazi Germany and *Star Wars* can be found in *Episode VII* where we see the same symbolism and colors of red, white, and black used to show us the First Order. It appears they also do a salute very similar to that of the Nazi party.

A curious idea to consider is the pursuit of a race war that Charles Manson predicted in the late 1960s that he dubbed "HELTER SKELTER." In this vision Manson had, the black community would destroy the white people only to find they needed Manson and his "Family" to lead them in an apocalyptic future. Manson would direct his Family members to conduct murders in the attempt to spark the race war by drawing various symbols and messages on the walls in the victims' blood such that the white people would think that black people did the crimes.

One such word that was used was "RISE" which Manson thought was a trigger word (taken from The

Beatles' song *Blackbird*). How curious is it that the command word "Rise" would appear often in the *Star Wars* saga as part of the dark side's story line?...

In *Episode III* we hear Darth Sidious tell Vader to "Rise" after he pledges allegiance to the dark side of the Force. In *Episode VI* the Emperor instructs Darth Vader to: "*Rise my friend.*"

Could it be that *Star Wars* is tapping into the same racial war madness that Charles Manson was witnessing?...

Were the racial tensions on the release of *Episode VII* part of some strange artifact of energy left behind from Manson's pursuit of HELTER SKELTER?...

Getting back to the topic of alien life; I believe that the Illuminati are showing us a future world through predictive programming in the hopes that it influences us to take the path necessary to get there. In Carl Jung's 1959 *Flying Saucers* he approached the investigation of UFOs as a component that was of psychological value and religious in nature. He and other analysts concluded that there is a mental, psychic component to the witnessing of aliens and UFOs, which supports the idea that there is an effort to instill the concept of extraterrestrial life forms into the pop culture-sphere. [20]

The final conclusion that they want us to believe is that further evolved beings from outer space will come to save us or somehow transform humanity to become something greater than what God intended. The reality is that alien "Messiahs" will merely be demons in disguise- which is what we see in *Episode VII* with the humanoid alien known as the Supreme Leader, Snoke.

Dr. Jacques Vallee wrote about this idea in *The Invisible College* in which he states that we are not dealing with visitations from space, but rather a control system. This control system is being used to create greater impact with society and drive many to become fascinated with space travel, supernatural phenomenon, and "new frontiers in consciousness." [59]

This is precisely why we are seeing tales like *Star Wars* being produced and reinforced on a regular, repeating basis. Our culture is *obsessed* with this tale, and Disney is seeking to instill messages through this readily-consumable medium. Carl Jung said that Christianity's "fatal flaw" was not allowing a "dark side" and advocated for a fourth dimension of the Trinity: Lucifer. [20]

So it seems that the religion of the future seeks to incorporate the "dark side of the Force" as an option; similar to the decisions presented to young Anakin Skywalker.

When we hear conspiracy theorists speak of a New World Order, we are indeed looking at a "One World Order" in which *everyone* worships a cosmic Force as a creative consciousness.

One of the steps necessary to take us down this path is the destruction of the family unit. We witness this process in *Star Wars* as well as many Disney tales. All of these tales depict children without parents. Sometimes the children witness the death of their parents; other times they've been absent for a long period of time.

An example is in *Episode II* when Jango Fett is beheaded by Mace Windu in front of his son, Boba Fett. In *Episode VI* we watch a sad Ewok witness the passing of an elder that appears to be his father. A more explicit example is in *Episode VI* when Obi-Wan Kenobi instructs Luke to actually kill *his own father*.

The exclusion of the parents is done on purpose. I believe it is done in order to traumatize the character, or the actual children watching the film.

These tragedies condition the victim to drop their resistance and cooperate with this blurred version of reality and fantasy. Cathy O'Brien details her time as a victim of this exact practice in *Trance: Formation of*

America where they forced her to watch *The Wizard of Oz* and *Alice in Wonderland*. [60] These films were utilized by her mind control handlers in order to disrupt her grasp of reality and allow them to continue their ritualistic abuse.

We also see Anakin Skywalker removed from his home as a young boy in order to prepare him to become a Jedi Knight warrior. He is separated from his mother, only to reunite with her as she takes her final breaths several years later.

This was foreshadowed in *Episode I* when Yoda tells Anakin that fear is the path to the dark side and the fear of losing his mother would lead to anger, hate, and suffering. Yoda's ominous last words to Anakin at the Council meeting are: "*I sense much fear in you...*" The traumatic death-separation is further reinforced when in *Episode III* we witness the death of Padme- the mother to Anakin's children.

We also saw traumatic mortality considerations in *Episode VII* when the Supreme Leader tells Kylo Ren that he *must* kill his father, Han Solo (which he eventually fulfills, showing the power of mind control the handlers have over their subjugates).

This same concept is demonstrated in the *Harry Potter* stories where children are taken to a school that teaches them the *same* supernatural powers of the occult we've spoken of already: alchemy, levitation, divination, genetic abilities, etc. (again- we see the concept of "light arts" and "dark arts" in these stories).

It is clear that the predictive programming in the Illuminati agenda is showing us a future world devoid of family unit structure as well as the annihilation of traditional religions. Instead, we see a world of individuals seeking to become god-like through their own abilities and harnessing powers of light and dark through contact with a universal consciousness and supernatural powers. The Luciferian doctrine is hard to deny once you open your eyes to the messages.

All of these things would make Aleister Crowley proud because some of his main goals were to destroy Christianity and pursue the empowerment of the individual and his or her Will. Others before me have noted the Crowley influences found within the *Star Wars* trilogy, so this isn't something I've alone come to my own conclusion on.

For instance, Crowley's secret name in the Ordo Templi Orientis magical order was supposedly "Phoenix." Not only is the phoenix symbolic of the final stage of alchemy (the fully enlightened individual), but it is also depicted as the symbol of the Rebel Alliance. Again we can associate the rebellious fallen angel with the "heroes" of this tale- the Rebel Alliance who are represented by the phoenix.

In Crowley's *Book of the Law* (which was dictated to him by a disembodied spirit called Aiwass- which some claim is translated as "Lucifer"), we hear him speak of the Obeah and the Wanga as the work of the wand & sword. Crowley instructed the initiate that they should learn and teach these, which is what we see Obi-Wan Kenobi doing in *Star Wars*- drawing the analogy of Obeah with Obi and Wanga with Wan. The astute theorists rightfully point out that the light saber is capable of being a wand one moment and a sword the next.

Another teacher from *Star Wars* is Yoda who Crowley references when he compares the dwarf to the Holy Guardian Angel in the *New Comment*:

But the "Small Person" of Hindu mysticism, the Dwarf insane yet crafty of many legends in many lands, is also this same "Holy Ghost", or Silent Self of a man, or his Holy Guardian Angel.

He is almost the "Unconscious" of Freud, unknown, unaccountable, the silent Spirit, blowing "whither it listeth, but thou canst not tell whence it cometh or whither it goeth". It

91

commands with absolute authority when it appears at all, despite conscious reason and judgment. [61]

When Crowley references the Holy Guardian Angel as *"the dwarf insane, yet crafty,"* he is regarding it as the source of true wisdom, much like we see in *Star Wars* as Yoda guides Luke Skywalker to his destiny, or "True Will."

We also hear about this concept of the Will in *Episode I* when Anakin was said to be the one to bring balance to the Force. At a Jedi Council meeting we hear Qui-Gon Jinn state:

"...finding him was the Will of the Force."

For those that aren't familiar; Crowley created his religion of Thelema based on the disembodied voice of his "Holy Guardian Angel" named Aiwass; similar to Yoda's disembodied voice heard in *Episode VII: The Force Awakens* when Rey touches Luke Skywalker's lightsaber and has flashbacks to its previous experiences.

We witness the guiding forces of spirits in *Star Wars* through Yoda and Obi-Wan Kenobi as they guide Luke Skywalker through the steps needed to battle Darth Vader and the Empire- akin to crossing the Abyss which is what Crowley talked about for the purpose of the Holy Guardian Angel:

It should never be forgotten for a single moment that the central and essential work of the Magician is the attainment of the Knowledge and Conversation of the Holy Guardian Angel. Once he has achieved this he must of course be left entirely in the hands of that Angel, who can be invariably and inevitably relied upon to lead him to the further great step— crossing of the Abyss and the attainment of the grade of Master of the Temple. [62]

When we see Luke Skywalker's right hand severed in *Episode V*, we could easily confer that his journey into the Abyss (aka Da'ath, or Darth Vader) was a failed attempt. In *Episode VI*, we hear Yoda warn Luke that the dark side is the shortcut, which is precisely what the occultists believe the Abyss represents on the Tree of Life!

Crowley warned of this process when he stated that one needs to be fully prepared to "confront Choronzon," and Luke was apparently not ready. We confirm this when we see the next film, *Episode VI*, where Luke faces Vader once again but this time removes Vader's right hand. The purpose in showing us the removal of the right hand is that the only path one can take to achieve enlightenment is that of the antinomian left hand path.

This left hand path concept is one that many occultists and ancient societies have understood. It is one in which the ancient Hindu followers have known for some period of time- further suggesting the eastern religious aspects of *Star Wars*. We can read literature on this idea and verify that the path of the left hand is considered one of darkness and destruction, but one that is required for full transformation:

> *The creative and productive aspect of the cosmic process is signified by the right hand, by the color white, and by the two goddesses Uma and Gauri (in whom Shakti appears as Prakashatmika, "she who is light and manifestation").*
>
> *The second aspect, that of conversion and return (exitus, reditus), is signified by the left hand, by the color black, and by the dark, destructive goddesses Durga and Kali. Thus, according to the Mahakala-Tantra, when the left and right hands are in equilibrium we experience samsara, but when the left hand prevails, we find liberation. [33]*

How ironic is it that Luke achieves full "balance" of the Force when he is attacked by the Emperor's

"Force Lightning," which is analogous to the lightning bolt that depicts that path down the Kabbalah Tree of Life (which contains the Abyss and Da'at sephirot)?

In Crowley's *The Equinox, Vol. 3, No. 1*, he describes an experience of approaching the Abyss, which features a couple similarities to Luke's time approaching Darth Vader in *Episode VI*, including the lightning bolt attack:

> *I was stricken as a bird by the bolt of the thunderer; I was pierced as the thief by the Lord of the Garden.* [63]

Also, before that verse we see something of interest that the reader will readily see as the plot from *Episode VI* as well:

> *I trembled at Thy coming, O my God, for They messenger was more terrible than the **Death-star**.* [63]

This makes sense in that *Return of the Jedi* shows Darth Vader merely transporting Luke to the Emperor. Vader is simply a messenger used to get Luke into the snares of the Emperor in the attempt to change him to the dark side. Back in *Episode IV* we heard Darth Vader tell Admiral Motti that he *was indeed* "more terrible than the **Death-star**":

> *Don't be too proud of this technological terror you've constructed. The ability to destroy a planet is insignificant next to the power of the Force.*

The journey that Luke Skywalker takes is not only that which seeks to "balance the Force," but also enlighten him to discover his true self. When Crowley describes a process of enlightenment, he mentions the necessary step of ego destruction; a process he calls the Night of Pan.

94

The language used to describe this process draws analogies to many of the concepts of *Star Wars:* duality, energy, death, and rebirth. In Crowley's *The Book of Lies* he describes it as such:

> *O! the heart of N.O.X. the Night of Pan.*
> *PAN: Duality: Energy: Death.*
> *Death: Begetting: the supporters of O!*
> *To beget is to die; to die is to beget.*
> *Cast the Seed into the Field of Night.*
> *Life and Death are two names of A.*
> *Kill thyself.*
> *Neither of these alone is enough.* [64]

Another reference to the Night of Pan (N.O.X.) is described in Crowley's *Liber VII*:

> *Ascend in the flame of the pyre, O my soul! Thy God is like the cold emptiness of the utmost heaven, into which thou radiatest thy little light.*
> *When Thou shall know me, O empty God, my flame shall utterly expire in Thy great N. O. X.* [64]

What makes this of particular interest to the *Star Wars* Universe is that Darth Vader's armor is cremated in a pyre at the end of *Episode VI*. In *Episode IV* we see Luke's adopted parents also being cremated in a pyre. Again, this is an ancient Hindu practice, as well as pagan cultures such as the early Romans and the Vikings during their period of Norse paganism. We can see this with the modern day Burning Man festival where a giant wicker man is burned in the desert in effigy of a mock sacrifice (*note that Count Dooku was played by Christopher Lee who was in the 1973 version of *Wicker Man*- a film about the same subject).

This ritual goes back to the Druids who conducted the same practice, which is *also* seen at the Bohemian Grove Cremation of Care ceremony on an annual basis. This Cremation of Care ceremony conducts a mock child sacrifice to the giant owl deity and is attended by politicians, businessmen, and entertainers.

The idea of a universal force or global consciousness is one that I disagree with because I don't comprehend the logic behind it. Their argument is that our world was created from a source of energy that had no intentionality or purpose for creating mankind. This energetic force would have no reason or desire to created humanity if that were the case.

To me it seems that there *must* be a God from which a world was created; not just some impersonal energy. Even scientists believe the universe is approximately 13.8 billion years old (based on the age of the oldest star), begging the question of who exactly created it. I can't reconcile the idea that a generic force kick-started the universe and just so happened to create mankind as part of the process. Of course, these are all debatable and personal beliefs, but it is the only way I can make sense of it.

The fact that occultists like Aleister Crowley subscribed to many of the same beliefs we see from the thread of pantheism, Luciferianism, eastern mysticism, Buddhism, Hinduism, Wicca, Satanists, and *Star Wars*; it begs the question of all these members being on the same "team" or at least deriving from the same inspiration. In fact, there now exists a religion called Jediism that is based on Lucas works of science fiction— echoing similarities to sci-fi author L. Ron Hubbard and his creation of the Church of Scientology.

I believe that Joseph Campbell was accurate in his assessment of ancient teachers and recurring lessons being presented in different fashions:

"The old teachers knew what they were saying. Once we have

learned to read again their symbolic language, it requires no

more than the talent of an anthologist to let their teaching be

heard. But first we must learn the grammar of the symbols, and

as a key to this mystery I know of no better modern tool than

psychoanalysis." [8]

In Hinduism, man can become divine by realizing divine, and this is what we find the characters of *Star Wars* doing when they reach out to the mystic powers of the Force. The followers of transcendental meditation also believe in the idea of gurus teaching others to focus mental powers in order to levitate, walk through walls, or even fly.

It's of no surprise that our modern day entertainment repeatedly bombards us with characters that have hidden powers or a "further evolved" state of being. I believe the entertainment industry is trying to influence us to reach out to this ethereal realm on our own in order to fall under the influence of a Luciferian force that seeks to deceive us.

As Father Seraphim Rose warned us, this is no different than black magic where you enter into a contract with an unknown entity. This appeals to the youth because Aleister Crowley ushered in the new age; the Aeon of Horus. This age promised to be one in which the crowned and conquering child reigned supreme. The youth like the idea of an impersonal Force being "god" because it allows many freedoms since it is not the relationship one would have with God the Father who requires one to devote time, energy, and patience into the relationship.

Like most science fiction films, *Star Wars* pushes the predictive programming of a future world in which Christianity is obsolete. Religions are not specifically mentioned in the tale, but the attributes of the Force resemble those of Crowley's amalgamation of eastern mysticism, Hinduism, Kabbalism, alchemy, and other esoteric studies. Aleister Crowley once called Christianity the "curse of the world" so it seems that the universe of *Star Wars* would be a place he would be most comfortable in.

> *"In this aeon the emphasis is on the self or will, not on anything external such as Gods and priests."*-Aleister Crowley, *The Book of the Law* [38]

I don't know that I'd go so far as to suggest that we should stop watching these films simply because they have these messages hidden in them. I'd rather think it's possible to watch them and enjoy them on the surface without allowing the ideals to influence our behaviors. Perhaps we could even find some redeeming or motivational qualities in them if we reconsidered our analysis.

The difficult aspect of this is in the messages and symbols that speak to us on a subconscious level, which is a far more insidious indoctrination than we can fathom. I believe that becoming aware of this agenda is enough to break the hypnotic spell; although many of us may not be strong enough to resist it; arguing for the point that maybe we *shouldn't* even expose ourselves to the deception.

I've personally been a fan of the *Star Wars* saga for my entire life so I don't anticipate that I will fully unplug from these stories entirely. The decision to continue watching these films is going to be up to the reader to decide.

Please just bear in mind that the truth is hidden in plain sight, and that *Star Wars* is a tale that influences many to obsess over a fictional world to the point that they subscribe to this fantasy as reality…

All the gods of the pagans are demons. -Psalms 95:5

Special Thanks:

God, family, and friends for the opportunity and support to be in the position I'm at today.

All the conspiracy theorists out there trying to keep the message alive; even in the face of adversity and denial from so many doubters.

Peter B. for his assist with Joseph Campbell's Monomyth.

Dr. Kim for support and motivation to keep progressing into this dark territory.

Chris W., Jason C., and Michael H. for opening my eyes to the Ancient Aliens deception.

Ken A. for more Star Wars references and general conspiracy theorizing.

The entire Illuminati "Watcher" community for their comments, questions, and support!!!

Bibliography

1]   J. McLauchlin, "Star Wars' $4 Billion Price Tag Was the Deal of the Century," [Online]. Available: http://www.wired.com/2015/12/disney-star-wars-return-on-investment/. [Accessed 15 08 2016].

2]   AP, "Army Will Close Child-Care Center," 16 Nov 1987. [Online]. Available: http://www.nytimes.com/1987/11/16/us/army-will-close-child-care-center.html. [Accessed 23 09 2016].

3]   L. Goldston, "Outpost-of-Freedom," [Online]. Available: http://www.outpost-of-freedom.com/aquino01.htm. [Accessed 23 09 2016].

4]   J. a. F. F. Hanshaw, Weird Stuff 2.

5]   P. R. L. Monica, "CNN Money," [Online]. Available: http://money.cnn.com/2006/01/24/news/companies/disney_pixar_deal/. [Accessed 08 09 2016].

6]   S. Schou, "EW.com," [Online]. Available: http://www.ew.com/article/2012/12/21/walt-disney-completes-lucasfilm-acquisition. [Accessed 08 09 2016].

7]   B. Child, "The Guardian," [Online]. Available: https://www.theguardian.com/film/2015/dec/31/george-lucas-attacks-retro-star-wars-the-force-awakens. [Accessed 08 09 2016].

8]   J. Campbell, The Hero With a Thousand Faces, Princeton University, 2004.

9]   J. Selvin, "Altamont: The Rolling Stones, the Hells Angels, and the Inside Story of Rock's Darkest Day," Harper Collins, 2016.

10]   Wikipedia, "Wikipedia- Marianne Faithfull," 23 09 2016. [Online]. Available: https://en.wikipedia.org/wiki/Marianne_Faithfull.

11]   J. a. F. F. Hanshaw, Weird Stuff: Operation Culture Creation, 2013.

12]   M. Pasi, Aleister Crowley and the Temptation of Politics.

13]   M. Phillips, High On Arrival, Simon & Schuster, 2009.

14]   A. Gorightly, The Shadow Over Santa Susana, Creation Books, 2009.

15]   C. O. a. M. Phillips, Trance: Formation of America, Reality Marketing, 2005.

16]   "LDS Living," [Online]. Available: http://www.ldsliving.com/How-Star-Wars-was-Influenced-by-a-Mormon/s/80835. [Accessed 08 09 2016].

17]   J. Baxter, George Lucas: A Biography, HarperCollins, 2016.

18]   P. McDonald, "Star Wars Heresies: Interpreting the Themes, Symbols, and Philosophies of Ep I, II, and III," 2013.

19]   Wikipedia, "The Force," [Online]. Available: https://en.wikipedia.org/wiki/The_Force_(Star_Wars). [Accessed 23 09 2016].

20]   F. S. Rose, Orthodoxy and the Religion of the Future, 4th ed., Saint Herman, 1997.

21]   L. Wright, Going Clear, 2013: Knopf Doubleday Publishing Group.

22]   D. K. A. G. a. M. L. Zimmerman, The Complete Idiot's Guide to Wicca and Witchcraft, 3rd ed., Penguin Group, 2006.

23]   C. Taylor, "Mashable," 27 09 2014. [Online]. Available: http://mashable.com/2014/09/27/star-wars-myths-gary-kurtz/#xqCtISDsfqqF. [Accessed 08 09 2016].

[24] F. Barrett, "The Magus," 1801.

[25] "Holy Bible," King James Version.

[26] A. Bailey, Problems of Humanity, Lucis, 1964.

[27] H. Blavatsky, Isis Unveiled, The Lucis Trust.

[28] M. Booth, The Secret History of the World, The Overlook Press, 2010.

[29] Wikipedia, "Jungian Archetypes," [Online]. Available: https://en.wikipedia.org/wiki/Jungian_archetypes. [Accessed 26 09 2016].

[30] I. Weishaupt, "IlluminatiWatcher," [Online]. Available: http://illuminatiwatcher.com/decoding-illuminati-symbolism-mark-beast-x/.

[31] A. Crowley, Little Essays Towards Truth, 1938.

[32] P. Levenda, The Dark Lord: H.P. Lovecraft, Kenneth Grant, and the Typhonian Tradition in Magic, Ibis Press, 2013.

[33] S. E. P. Flowers, Lords of the Left-Hand Path: Forbidden Practices and Spiritual Heresies, Inner Traditions/Bear & Company, 2012.

[34] K. Ammi, "TrueFreeThinker," [Online]. Available: http://www.truefreethinker.com/articles/everything-i-know-about-occult-i-learned-watching-star-wars. [Accessed 01 11 2016].

[35] D. J. Satinover, The Empty Self: C.G. Jung & the Gnostic Transformation of the Modern Identity, Revised Edition ed., Hamewith Books, 1996.

[36] R. A. Barlett, Real Alchemy: A Primer of Practical Alchemy, Nicolas-Hays, 2009.

[37] A. Crowley, The Confessions of Aleister Crowley: An Autohagiography.

38]   A. Crowley, The Book of the Law.

39]   M. Heiser, "The Myth of a Sumerian 12th Planet," [Online]. Available: http://www.sitchiniswrong.com/nibirunew.pdf. [Accessed 29 09 2016].

40]   Wikipedia, "Erich von Daniken," [Online]. Available: https://en.wikipedia.org/wiki/Erich_von_Däniken. [Accessed 29 09 2016].

41]   Wikipedia, "Giorgio Tsoukalos," [Online]. Available: https://en.wikipedia.org/wiki/Giorgio_A._Tsoukalos. [Accessed 29 09 2016].

42]   M. Sula, "Atlantis Ho!," [Online]. Available: http://www.chicagoreader.com/chicago/atlantis-ho/Content?oid=923072. [Accessed 29 09 2016].

43]   "Donald Marshall Revolution," [Online]. Available: http://donaldmarshallrevolution.com. [Accessed 29 09 2016].

44]   Astral7ight, "Astral7ight," [Online]. Available: http://astral7ight.blogspot.com/p/vril-type-3.html. [Accessed 29 09 2016].

45]   *Star Wars: Episode III Revenge of the Sith DVD commentary featuring George Lucas.* [Film]. 2005.

46]   Wookieepedia, "Kaminoan," [Online]. Available: http://starwars.wikia.com/wiki/Kaminoan. [Accessed 29 09 2016].

47]   M. W. Cooper, Behold a Pale Horse, Light Technology Publishing, 1991.

48]   H. Blavatsky, The Secret Doctrine, Online Edition ed., Theosophical University.

49]   W. Ramsey, "Illuminati's Ideology of Enslavement," [Online]. Available: http://www.henrymakow.com/adolf_hitler_and_aleister_crow.html. [Accessed 29 09 2016].

50]   L. Kasten, "The Nazi/ET Connection: The War for Planet Earth," [Online]. Available: http://www.bibliotecapleyades.net/vida_alien/warheaven_warearth12.htm. [Accessed 29 09 2016].

[51] J. Parsons, "The Book of the Antichrist," [Online]. Available: http://hermetic.com/parsons/the-book-of-the-antichrist.html. [Accessed 29 09 2016].

[52] Wiki, "Project Blue Beam," [Online]. Available: http://rationalwiki.org/wiki/Project_Blue_Beam. [Accessed 29 09 2016].

[53] Express, "World on brink of being told 'aliens EXIST' after NASA 'hints at announcement'," [Online]. Available: http://www.express.co.uk/news?utm_source=DY&utm_medium=DY _Desktop&utm_content=DY_Slot1&utm_campaign=DY_Recommend ed%20overlay. [Accessed 29 09 2016].

[54] M. Wall, "Signs of Alien Life Will Be Found by 2025, NASA's Chief Scientist Predicts," [Online]. Available: http://www.space.com/29041-alien-life-evidence-by-2025-nasa.html. [Accessed 29 09 2016].

[55] M. Ryan, "'Star Wars' Prequels Were Mapped Out By George Lucas & Lawrence Kasdan In 1981: Exclusive Excerpt From 'The Making Of Star Wars: Return of the Jedi'," [Online]. Available: http://www.huffingtonpost.com/2013/05/22/star-wars-prequels-return-of-the-jedi_n_3313793.html. [Accessed 13 10 2016].

[56] D. Tumminia, Alien Worlds: Social and Religious Dimensions of Extraterrestrial Contact (Religion and Politics), Syracuse University Press, 2007.

[57] A. Crowley, "Crowley Book 4," [Online]. Available: http://hermetic.com/crowley/book-4/app2.html. [Accessed 24 10 2016].

[58] E. v. Eckartshausen, The Cloud Upon the Sanctuary.

[59] J. Vallee, The Invisible College, 1975.

[60] C. O'Brien, Trance: Formation of America.

[61] A. Crowley, The Old and New Commentaries to Liber Al Vel Legis.

[62] A. Crowley, Magick Without Tears, Falcon Press, 1982.

[63] A. Crowley, The Equinox.

[64] Wikipedia, "Night of Pan," [Online]. Available:
https://en.wikipedia.org/wiki/Night_of_Pan. [Accessed 13 10 2016].

[65] Forum, "Thelemic References in the Star Wars Trilogy," [Online].
Available: http://forum.forteantimes.com/index.php?threads/thelemic-references-in-the-star-wars-trilogy.11594/. [Accessed 01 10 2016].

A GRAND UNIFIED CONSPIRACY THEORY:
THE ILLUMINATI, ANCIENT ALIENS AND POP CULTURE

A Grand Unified Conspiracy Theory: The Illuminati, Ancient Aliens, and Pop Culture:

This is a comprehensive beginner's guide to ALL things conspiracy!

'A Grand Unified Conspiracy Theory: The Illuminati, Ancient Aliens, and Pop Culture' is a culmination project of several years of research and taking notes on taboo and fringe subjects from various theorists, philosophies, and academic walks of life. I'm a website publisher for conspiracy theories and the exposure that I've had to these topics gives me a fresh perspective and clarity of these sometimes confusing and offensive topics. I focus a lot of the material on the philosophy of David Icke, so if you wanted an independent third party assessment on why he thinks reptilian shape shifters control our planet (and why he could be correct); this is the book for you!

I explore links between all of the Illuminati conspiracy

theories, the music, film, and entertainment industry's infiltration, and brainwashing symbolism found in all of these venues (e.g. the All Seeing Eye, pyramids, etc.). Ancient cultures, Nazis and occult worship still play a key role in today's control system, and I provide insight into these topics, including a never before released review of a controversial and banned documentary of Princess Diana's murder. This film has never been released and I was able to watch a copy of it and review its findings.

More original theories are presented such as Rihanna's occult origins, red dragons and their symbolism, and the Illuminati eugenics program being deployed through a transhuman robotic agenda. I also explain how David Icke's theories of the Moon Matrix and Saturn Worship operate to manipulate us into a false reality.

I wrap the book up with a conclusion of what actually works out of all this mess. It includes an assessment of David Icke's reptilian shape shifters explained through a legitimate cognitive style model theory in academia called 'Adaption-Innovation' theory.

Available on Amazon.com, iTunes, and the Gumroad.com "IsaacW" store with signed paperback copies. Also available: audiobook on Audible through Amazon or iTunes; narrated by Eric Burns.

SACRIFICE: MAGIC BEHIND THE MIC

This is the ONLY book that reveals the Illuminati & occult agenda behind the hip hop music industry in *SACRIFICE: MAGIC BEHIND THE MIC.* You'll learn all about the secrets behind Jay-Z's magical hand symbol, the Illuminati blood sacrifices of Tupac and Aaliyah, and how the occult magick practitioners like Aleister Crowley secretly harness the energy of the entire music fanbase. This is the book featured on *The HigherSide Chats* podcast and Freeman's *The Free Zone.*

Learn about the mind control and demonic possession that plagues today's most popular rap and R&B artists as you acquire the skills necessary to become aware of the plan the music industry has to instill occultist Aleister Crowley's ushering of the New Age of Horus.

Explore the dark corners of conspiracy theories revolving around the murder of musicians for the ancient practice of sacrifice to the blood thirsty pagan gods and selling of one's soul in exchange for fame and fortune. The codex for decoding all of the major Illuminati symbols is revealed in the Appendix that provides rich detail of symbols such as the All Seeing

Eye, black cube of Saturn, and much more.

· Origins of hip hop
· How the Illuminati manipulates the black culture through an industrial prison complex and negative messages in rap music
· The use of magical spells used in lyrics and music videos
· Demonic possession and MKULTRA mind control
· Eminem, Rihanna, and Jay-Z's **'Rain Man'** demonic entity
· The reason Tupac, BIG, Aaliyah, Left Eye, ODB and Michael Jackson were murdered
· Death Row Records involvement with the CIA and Illuminati
· The black Skull & Bones secret society known as 'The Boule'
· How an FBI COINTELPRO secret program assassinated black leaders with positive messages
    · Prince and Jay-Z predicting 9/11 & Beyonce channeling the spirit of Sasha Fierce
· Dr. Dre's Illuminati power move to become rap's first billionaire
· The crossover into the Age of Aquarius with pop stars like Katy Perry, Miley Cyrus, & Bieber
· Kabbalah secrets in the music industry
· DMX, Kanye West, and Lauryn Hill all revealed the true nature of the music industry
· …and MUCH more!

Available on Amazon.com, iTunes, and the Gumroad.com "IsaacW" store with signed paperback copies. Also available: author narrated audiobook on Audible.com through Amazon or iTunes.

KUBRICK'S CODE

In this book, author and independent researcher Isaac Weishaupt presents hundreds of images and analysis from Stanley Kubrick's most popular films- *2001: A Space Odyssey, A Clockwork Orange, The Shining*, and *Eyes Wide Shut*.

Learn all about the conspiracy theory of the secret message Kubrick tried to convey about the occult and the Illuminati before his untimely passing. This book lays out examples of scenes and covertly placed messages and themes within Kubrick's films that supports the idea he was privy to the Illuminati secret agenda.

The full-color images taken directly from the films are explained with analysis that suggests Kubrick knew much more than many people believe. This book contains some adult themes, but some images (specifically the *Eyes Wide Shut* scenes) have been edited to ensure no full nudity.

BONUS VIDEO DOCUMENTARY

If you order this ebook PDF through the IlluminatiWatcher Gumroad store you'll ALSO receive the two-hour companion video that provides more images and clips from *2001: A Space Odyssey, A Clockwork*

Orange, The Shining, and *Eyes Wide Shut* (these are extended versions NOT available on YouTube).

KUBRICK'S CODE is available on Amazon.com, iTunes, and the Gumroad.com "IsaacW" store with signed paperback copies and DVDs of the KUBRICK'S CODE video.

Also available: author narrated audiobook on Audible.com through Amazon or iTunes.

ALICE IN ROCKY HORRORLAND:

ENTERTAINMENT'S PURSUIT OF THE TRANSHUMAN DESERT APOCALYPSE

Get four books in one epic collection!

The project referred to as *Alice in Rocky Horrorland: Entertainment's Pursuit of the Transhuman Desert Apocalypse* is a compilation of various research efforts to expose the entertainment industry's attempt to implant certain messages and themes into humanity's subconscious via pop culture.

Many of us have participated in these events; whether it was enjoying the tale of *Alice in Wonderland* and her occult initiation into the underground or the sexualization of the androgynous aliens of *Rocky Horror Picture Show* and their dance across the Abyss (you didn't think the Time Warp song was just in good humor did you?...); you're sure to change the way you view these works of art after considering the evidence that lies within.

ALICE IN ROCKY HORRORLAND:

ENTERTAINMENT'S PURSUIT OF THE
TRANSHUMAN DESERT APOCALYPSE

ISAAC WEISHAUPT

The Illuminati end game is total annihilation and this New World Order will be established through their evolution of consciousness which craftily guides the unaware through New Age agendas found within Paulo Coelho's best-selling tale: *The Alchemist.*

The ultimate apocalypse will be the final push of man into the digital substrate known as transhumanism, where the final Mark of the Beast will be imprinted on all those who aren't awake to the agenda...

ALICE IN ROCKY HORRORLAND is available on Amazon.com, iTunes, and the Gumroad.com "IsaacW" store with signed paperback copies.

Also available: author narrated audiobook on Audible.com through Amazon or iTunes.

Made in the USA
Middletown, DE
18 July 2021

44283990R00071